The Sweat Lodge is for Everyone

We are all related

The non-Native's guide to building, participating in, and benefiting from Native American Sweat Lodge ceremonies

The Sweat Lodge is for Everyone

Irene McGarvie

Ancient Wisdom Publishing
a division of Nixon-Carre Ltd., Toronto, ON

Copyright © 2009 by Irene McGarvie

Library and Archives Canada Cataloguing in Publication

McGarvie, Irene, 1957-
    The sweat lodge is for everyone : we are all related / Irene McGarvie.

ISBN 978-0-9737470-6-5

    1. Sweatbaths. 2. Indians of North America--Rites and ceremonies. 3. Indians of North America--Religion. I. Title.
E98.S94M33 2009   299.7'138
C2008-906340-6

Published by:
Ancient Wisdom Publishing
A division of Nixon-Carre Ltd.
P.O. Box 92533
Carlton RPO
Toronto, Ontario, M5A 4N9

www.learnancientwisdom.com
www.nixon-carre.com

Distributed by Ingram

Disclaimer:
This publication is designed to provide accurate and authoritative information. It is sold with the understanding that the publishers are not engaged in rendering legal, medical or other professional advice. If medical or other expert assistance is required, the services of a competent professional should be sought. The information contained herein represents the experiences and opinions of the author, but the author is not responsible for the results of any action taken on the basis of information in this work, nor for any errors or omissions.

General Notice:
Any product names used in this book are for identification purposes only and may be registered trademarks, or trade names of their respective owners. The author, Irene McGarvie, and the publisher, Ancient Wisdom Publishing (a division of Nixon-Carre Ltd.) disclaim any and all rights in those marks.

Printed and bound in the USA

"All major religious traditions carry basically the same message, that is love, compassion and forgiveness ... the important thing is they should be part of our daily lives."

the Dalai Lama

This book is dedicated to

Dr. Neal Rzepkowski

"The One Who Poured the Water"

during my first sweat lodge ceremony.

With special thanks to all the people who helped with suggestions, encouragement and proofreading:

Jacqlyn Avis
Mike Morley
Sue Rogge
Sharon Russell

Contents

A great gift almost lost • Usurping a tradition? • Native American spirituality is not for sale • Nicholas Black Elk • Message from a 'winged one'

Who started the sweat lodge? • The mythology of heat, fire, and steam • The life cycle and rebirth • Sweat • Mayan sweat houses • The Russian Bania • The birth bania • The wedding bania • The death bania • The Russian bania comes to America • The Finnish sauna • The farmer who loved to take a sauna • Finnish immigrants bring the sauna to America • Sweden • Germany • Natives of the Pacific coast • The Ancient Greeks • The Roman Baths • Islam and the hammam • Ginn the spirit of the hammam • Women and the hammam

We fear what we don't understand • The Great Spirit • In harmoney with nature • The Standing People • The Stone People • The number 4 • The 7 Sacred Directions • The circle of life • Spiritual beings on a human journey • Balance • Male and female roles • Homosexuality • Children and Elders • Medicine bundles • The sacred pipe • The Pipe Ceremony • The Sundance • The Vision Quest • The Spirit Calling Ceremony • The Potlatch

We Are All Related

1

"All human beings come from a mother's womb. We are all the same part of one human family. We should have a clear realization of the oneness of all humanity.

All religions are essentially the same in their goal of developing a good human heart so that we may become better human beings."

The Dalai Lama

Generally, when we refer to the sweat lodge, particularly when we are talking about sweating as a spiritual practice, we are usually referring to the Native American sweat lodge, but there is evidence to indicate that almost every culture indulged in some form of sweat bathing since long before recorded history.

So who started it? Did the American Indians bring the sweat lodge ceremony with them from Asia many thousands of years ago when they crossed the Bering Strait into what is now North America? Or did we all just come up with the idea independently? We will never know for sure, but since science has conclusively proven that we are all descended from common ancestors, it is probably safe to assume that the sweat lodge is something that mankind has practiced since the beginning.

A great gift almost lost

Most people around the world have somehow forgotten the symbolism and spiritual lessons of the sweat lodge, and communal sweating has become more of a health practice or form of recreation than a spiritual ceremony, but deep down inside we all have the same need to connect with Spirit and with Mother Earth as our ancestors did.

Followers of Native American spirituality believe that the sweat lodge was a gift from the Great Spirit, a gift that can benefit us both spiritually and physically. I believe that it was a gift given to all of mankind, not something exclusively Native American.

Due to persecution from the government and the Christian church, during the 19th and 20th centuries, North American Native religious practices almost disappeared. The government and the church viewed ceremonies like the Sweat Lodge, the Sun Dance, and the Potlatch, with their sacred and religious implications, as threatening to their control of the Native people and banned their practice.

Fortunately some people, in spite of the risk of punishment, continued these practices in secret and thanks to them we have this knowledge available to us today. It is thanks primarily to the Lakota Sioux people, who stubbornly refused to allow their traditions to be wiped out, that the rest of us are now able to learn (or perhaps remember?) the lessons of the sweat lodge. As a result, when we refer to the sweat lodge ceremony we are usually talking about the traditional Lakota Sioux hot rock style sweat lodge.

Usurping a tradition?

It is important to mention a controversy that has developed regarding the sweat lodge. There are some Native people who resent the adoption of Native American religious ceremonies, such as the sweat lodge, by non-Natives, believing it to be one more attempt by the white man to steal or otherwise violate Native culture.

Considering the Native peoples' history of suffering terribly at the hands of European invaders I can certainly understand why they would feel that way, but the benefits of the sweat lodge are so great that I think it is totally inconsistent with traditional Native beliefs to keep this knowledge away from people who desperately need it, regardless of their ancestry.

Traditionally, Native spiritual practices were passed down, in an oral tradition, from the Elders. Those in the next generation were very carefully chosen to carry on the traditions after many years of observing the individual's character and after exhibiting evidence of being chosen by Spirit. But for the past 200 years, due to government interference and the influence of the "Christian" church, there have been less and less people able to hand down this oral tradition.

In recent years, due to the surge of interest in Native religious practices among both Natives and non-Natives, and the scarcity of Elders who can teach these practices, other people have begun teaching what was once strictly the domain of the elders. Most did so out of a sincere desire to help others, but unfortunately some had less noble goals.

Native religious practices were traditionally never done for money, primarily because it was not necessary to do so. The community was already providing for the Elders who were performing the ceremonies or providing the teaching. People would bring them food and firewood, not because they were getting paid to perform a job, rather simply because they were part of the community, and as such were valued and taken care of.

Unfortunately, it is a different world today, and even spiritual leaders require a source of income. I think it is perfectly appropriate to give a gift of money to a spiritual leader who has performed a ceremony or taught you something; similar to the concept of tithing in other religions, but this should be a gift, not a requirement.

In the words of Ed McGaa in his wonderful book **Mother Earth Spirituality**, "Native spirituality is not for sale".

Unfortunately, leading sweat lodge ceremonies has become something of an industry, where people with spurious claims to being "Medicine Men" or "Shaman" charge unwitting participants large sums of money to take part. This is not appropriate. Choosing to give a gift is one thing, but charging people for participating in a sweat lodge is not the traditional way.

I think the fact that people can get taken advantage of by these opportunists is an indication of how desperate we all are to become closer to Spirit, and hoping that the sweat lodge can provide us with a "direct line".

You might be asking yourself, by writing this book about the sweat lodge, am I not simply one of these opportunists hoping to make money out of people's spiritual hunger? If you think so, then you do not understand the economic realities of the publishing industry in the 21st century. Believe me when I say that I have no delusions that this book will be the next 'Harry Potter' or 'Da Vinci Code', and propel me toward wealth and fame.

So then, what do I, as a white woman, hope to achieve in writing this book? This book has two purposes for me:

- To explain this spiritual practice to other non-Natives as clearly as possible. I think that as an outsider I had many of the same questions as other non-Natives and can explain it from an outsider's perspective.

- To enhance my own understanding. In my experience, the best way to really understand something is to teach it to someone else.

There is no new knowledge. I do not pretend to have created any of the information in this book. The things we learn today or a hundred years from now are not truly new. They may be new to us, but the knowledge was always there, we are simply uncovering it again.

There is truth in all religions, it all comes from the

same source, and we are all part of that source. We are one. We are related to all creation.

Nicholas Black Elk

Back in the 1930's the great Lakota visionary and healer Nicholas Black Elk predicted that the day would come when all people would come together and acknowledge the unity of all humanity, our interdependence, and our dependence on Mother Earth. I think that the current surge in interest, on the part of non-Natives, toward traditional Native American spirituality is part of Black elk's prediction coming to pass.

Black Elk wanted the ancient ways to be remembered by his people, and all the people of the world regardless of their race, creed or color.

To learn more about this great man, I recommend the book *"Black Elk Speaks"* by John Neihardt, published by the University of Nebraska Press.

Message from a "Winged One"

When I am out in the bush I occasionally find feathers in my path, gifts from our brothers the "Winged Ones". One incident that was particularly significant for me took place when I was in the campsite at Lily Dale sitting meditating at a picnic table. The loud cry of a Blue Jay startled me and

I opened my eyes to find a beautiful Blue Jay feather lying directly in front of me on the picnic table.

This experience was one of the events that led me to write this book. Up until this point I had felt that there was a need for a book like this but considering the animosity that some Native Americans feel towards white people usurping their heritage, I did not want to offend anyone, and I thought that it was presumptuous of me to consider myself qualified to write such a book, but I felt conflicted because I truly believe that the sweat lodge can benefit everyone regardless of their ethnic background.

What was the Blue Jay trying to tell me when he gave me his feather? Since Blue Jays are known for their fearless (almost bullying nature) and their loud cry, I took his gift as a sign that it was time for me to be like the Blue Jay and speak out, be fearless, and take a stand, regardless of what other people might think.

I think that Black Elk would approve.

"*There can never be peace between nations until there is first known that true peace which is within the souls of men.*"

Black Elk

2

The Sweat Lodge Around the World

Who started the sweat lodge?

In one form or another, there is a form of sweat lodge or sweat bath in almost every culture. Its function goes beyond simply getting the body clean, although it performs that function very well. Throughout history the sweat bath provided a cure for illness, relief for aching muscles, a sense of community, and a spiritual/religious experience.

Since no one really knows who started the custom of ceremonial sweat bathing, and since the ritual, folklore, and even construction of sweat baths are so similar all over the world, I think that we can assume that they have been in use all the way back to our common ancestors.

There are slight differences in the ceremonies and style of construction in sweat lodges around the world, but the unique geographic, and environmental conditions, as well as the types of plant life available, can account for these differences. For example, Finnish people like their sweat bath hot and relatively dry, perhaps due to their colder climate, while Islamic hammam bathers further south prefer cooler, steamier sweat baths. The early Romans used both styles in their baths.

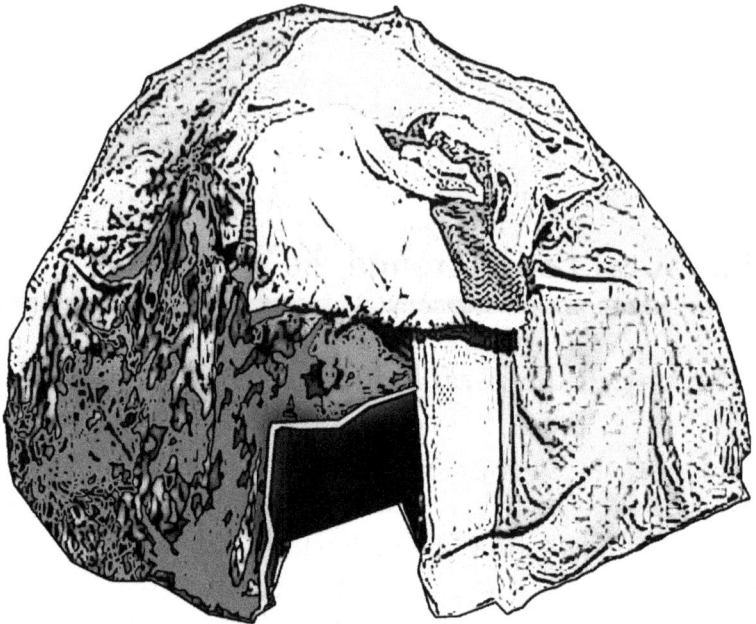

Some Native American bands build willow framed huts, while African tribes tend to build their huts from grass or mud, and the ancient Greeks and Romans built more elaborate structures made of stone. Some cultures chant, while others enjoy quiet meditation in the sweat bath. But regardless of whether we participate in traditional Native American sweat lodges or in a communal sweat ceremony on the other side of the world, the benefits to be derived are similar.

While it is true that, at first glance, some forms of sweat bathing seem to be more recreational than spiritual, I think if you look closely you will see that even the most hedonistic had some initial spiritual symbolism.

The Mythology of Heat, Fire, and Steam

Fire has always commanded respect. It symbolizes power, vigor and vitality. It represents the sun or the light of day - consciousness. In Greek mythology, Prometheus was credited with the founding of civilization by stealing fire from the gods and delivering it to humans.

Other cultures believed that fire was not stolen, but rather was a gift from God, and if fueled with choice firewood and tended to with appropriate ritual and respect, diseases and spiritual evils could be driven off. However, if treated disrespectfully, fire would engulf and destroy.

Fire is always moving, consuming, and changing. In the case of the sweat lodge ceremony, this characteristic of fire represents our desire to change something about ourselves.

In both the Judaic and the Christian traditions, God is often portrayed as fire, revealing himself to Moses as a burning bush, and as pillars of fire shining in heaven. Satan and the concept of burning in hell symbolize the destructive aspect of fire.

Water represents the unconscious, the unknown, and the mysterious. Our bodies are 2/3's water. While most of us have enough reserves that we can go a long time without food, we would only be able to live a few days without water. In addition to being vital for life, water is valued because of its ability to dissolve, purify and regenerate.

The sweat lodge, by utilizing the power of fire and water, became a sacred shrine. When it was discovered that rocks could absorb the power of fire (the heat) they also acquired spiritual significance. When water was splashed over heated rocks, the vapor produced became an instrument for the transfer of heat and another object of reverence, something powerful and holy -- the visible symbol of the Creator's Breath. The Finns call this vapor "loyly", or "spirit of life". Some American Indians call this spirit "Manitou". Regardless of what name it was given, people all over the world believed that this friendly spirit dwelled inside rocks and could be released through water vapor to penetrate the skins of the bathers and drive out sickness.

The Life Cycle and Rebirth

Another reason for the link between the sweat bath and spirituality is its association with birth and re-birth. A person absorbing the heat of a sweat bath symbolically re-enacts Creation, the merging of body and fire. The invigorating effect of the sweat bath, as well as its similarity to a womb or nest, made it a natural place for purification and rebirth rituals. The weary bather enters into the confines of the sweat lodge, sweats out physical, mental, emotional and spiritual impurities and emerges from the process refreshed and cleansed. Because of this symbolic re-birth, other rites of passage were often connected with sweat bathing, for example, rituals surrounding birth, adulthood, marriage and death.

Throughout history childbirth was a dangerous time for both mother and child. In many cultures women gave birth inside sweat lodges in order to be in the presence of benevolent spirits who, it was believed, would reduce the pains of childbirth and increase the chance of survival for both mother and child.

In Native American traditions, the warm, dark, moist environment inside the sweat lodge represents the womb of Mother Earth from whom we are all descended.

Sweat

The visible product of the combination of man and heat (the Creator) is sweat. Therefore, many primitive people believed that sweat was a powerful, magical substance that carried both spiritual and human powers. In some warrior societies young men would drink the sweat of renowned warriors so that they too might become strong and fearless.

Before a marriage, Russian peasants would sometimes concoct an aphrodisiac for the groom made with vodka and sweat from the bride-to-be.

Sweat is a prominent feature in several creation stories from around the world. In both Russian and Indian folklore there are stories about how the first people were created through drops of sweat falling from God in a sweat bath.

A Hindu tale about how the god Siva wiped the sweat away from his brow with a piece of cloth, then threw the cloth away, and out of this a girl was born, indicates that ancient Hindus believed that sweat carried the seeds of life.

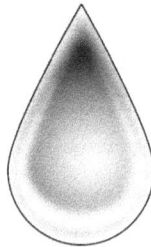

Mayan Sweat Houses - Temescal

The Mayan were an extremely advanced civilization who lived in the region that is now Southern Mexico and Central America from about 2600 BCE until their decline about 900 CE. Why this civilization declined is not fully understood, but by about 1200 CE they were taken over by the Toltecs/Aztecs who incorporated many Mayan practices including that of the sweathouse, which was a common part of ancient Mayan life. Excavations at ancient Mayan sites have uncovered sweathouse ruins believed to be over 1200 years old.

When the Spanish arrived in the area in the 16th century they were appalled at the elaborate bathing practices of the Aztec people. Spain was still entrenched in the dark ages of sanitation when bathing was considered unhealthy and unnecessary, and most Spanish chose not to bathe at all. Spain's Queen Isabella bragged that she had only bathed twice in her life, once when she was born and once when she married. Also, the Spaniards recognized that these bathing practices had some sort of powerful spiritual component and involved the worship of gods, so, with the encouragement of the Roman Catholic Church, they endeavoured to abolish these native bathing rituals.

The Russian Bania

The traditional Russian bania was an important part of Russian peasant life. In addition to being a great way to relax and get clean, it was an important social event. The bania figured prominently in all the traditional rituals surrounding birth, marriage and death.

One thing that differentiates the Russian bania from other sweathouses is the common use of alcohol, specifically vodka. In most cultures, the use of alcohol during a sweat is strongly discouraged, but in the bania it is very common to sip vodka, pour it on the rocks to create a slightly intoxicating steam, or to pour a little on the body as an astringent.

My husband and I had a wonderful time at a modern Russian bathhouse in Miami Beach. We weren't looking for a spiritual experience, rather just an interesting activity while we were on vacation. We were expecting to spend an hour or two, but it turned out to be a very memorable 8-hour event, and we were very sorry to leave that night when they closed.

At first it seemed a little intimidating. In the lobby, bunches of birch twigs hung from the ceiling, pieces of birch leaves and twigs were all over the floor. We could hear strange sounds, and we wondered what we had let ourselves in for. In the various rooms, people were alternately steaming themselves, taking turns whacking each other with bunches of birch twigs, and shocking themselves with buckets of ice water. There was a snack bar where you could get a sandwich, and a bar where you could get a shot of vodka. People were talking to each other, and it was obvious that this was a place where friends gathered to socialize. Of course, this being a public facility in the United States, everyone was wearing bathing suits.

Once we got over our initial apprehension, and decided to give it a try, we had a great time. We repeatedly steamed ourselves, froze ourselves, ate, drank, talked and were amazed to realize that we had stayed till closing time.

I realize that this was not exactly like a traditional Russian bania, and it certainly wasn't a spiritual or religious experience, but the socializing was great and the alternating hot and cold felt wonderful (once you got used to it). We had a great time and I'd love to have the opportunity to go again. Aside from having a lot of fun, it was so relaxing; our heads barely hit the pillow that night before we were asleep.

The Birth Bania

Since it was clean and warm, the bania was the perfect place for a Russian peasant woman to give birth. My use of the word "peasant" is not intended to be derogatory in any way, it simply refers to someone from the hardworking, rural, farming class that most of us descend from rather than the aristocratic ruling class.

The Russian midwife's job was to assist with the birth and to keep the Bannik from interfering. The Bannik was the spirit who lived in the bania, and unlike bath house spirits in other cultures, the Bannik was thought to be an evil spirit who could cause problems and needed to be appeased.

The best way to appease the Bannik was to keep the bania spotlessly clean and well stocked with firewood, water, and birch twigs, and to behave in a respectful manner. It was customary to greet the Bannik respectfully upon entering and leaving, and to make the sign of the cross for protection.

The Wedding Bania

The Russian Church reluctantly blessed the wedding bania as one of the few permissible pagan rituals. Probably because they realized that the practice was too strongly entrenched for them to be able to successfully eradicate it so it made more sense to incorporate it into the Christian rituals.

The ritual began the night before with both the bride and groom taking separate baths with their friends and family. Traditionally the groom's engagement gift to the bride was a new birch whisk and a piece of soap. The groom's pre-wedding bania tended to be more of a drunken party than a solemn ceremony, but the bride-to-be's bania was much more solemn and ritualistic.

Immediately after the wedding it was time for the new couple to take a sweat bath together. The custom was for the groom to lift his new wife over the threshold of the bania. (The reasoning behind this practice was that since the bania was also used as a place to give birth and since stillborn children were buried there, by lifting his new wife over the threshold this would prevent his first born from suffering the same fate.) As the new couple undressed and tossed water on the rocks, outside the wedding guests threw rocks at the bania to scare away the Bannik, thereby ensuring a happy marriage.

The Death Bania

To prepare a Russian soul for its next life, the body would be washed in the bania and placed in a coffin, a pillow would be stuffed with birch leaves and the coffin abundantly supplied with birch twigs.

After the burial the friends and family would bath together. This communal bathing helped the mourners to deal with their grief. Forty days after the death, (which was believed to be the length of time necessary for the soul to make its journey to the other world) it was customary for the friends and relatives to once again bathe together and drink toasts to the memory of the deceased.

The Russian bania comes to North America

Between 1880 and 1930 over three million people emigrated from Russia to the North America. They tended to live in large cities like New York, Chicago, and Montreal, in squalid apartments with no baths, working under difficult conditions. So wherever there was a high concentration of Russian immigrants an entrepreneur would be sure to open a public bania. The bania brought back fond memories of home and provided an important social gathering place.

The popularity of these Russian baths gradually declined as showers, or "rain baths" became popular. It is unfortunate that industrialized societies have little time for a leisurely Russian style bath.

This same situation has occurred in China in recent years, as their country rapidly becomes industrialized and traditional bathhouses close.

The Finnish Sauna

When most people think of sweat baths the first thing they think of is the traditional Finnish sauna. No other culture is so closely associated with sweat bathing, with good reason. Throughout history Finns used the sauna from birth to death. Children were born in the sauna, and old people were often brought there to die. Young couples starting out would build the sauna first and live in it while building their house.

The sauna was not a luxury for the Finns. Most of the people lived off the land - a difficult life in a country with a harsh climate and a very short growing season. Having a sauna after a long day of work relaxes the muscles, cleanses the body, and clears the mind. As well, since depression is a major problem for people in northern regions during the winter, nothing can brighten the cold dark days of winter like time in the sauna.

Taking a sauna clothed was simply not done since clothing interferes with sweating. Attitudes toward nudity are relaxed in Finland and other Scandinavian countries so it was common for men and women to bathe together, whole families with small children playing on the floor, and adults taking the higher, hotter benches.

The sauna was also an important social event. It was common for neighbors to take turns preparing the sauna. When it was ready, they would knock on their neighbors' doors and shout, "Come, the bath is ready!"

The Finns believed that a good sweat could cure almost anything, hence the old Finnish saying "The sauna is the poor man's apothecary."

Even today, there are strict rules of propriety when taking a sauna. No inappropriate behavior is tolerated. There is an old saying, which sums up the Finnish attitude toward the sauna, "In the sauna one must conduct oneself as you would in church."

Years ago when I lived in north western Ontario I was invited to use the old log sauna that belonged to some friends. The husband was Finnish and the sauna was one that his father had built when he first came to Canada. It was located near the water's edge, which made it very convenient for hauling water and also for having quick dips in the lake. It was big enough to accommodate a family and so it took many hours to really heat properly by Finnish standards.

Every Saturday the fire would be started, many pails of water would be hauled from the lake, and the old wringer washer would be rolled inside. By the time the laundry was all hanging neatly on the clothesline outside the sauna would be ready.

I can still remember the smell of the cedar logs, the heat of the wood fire, and how wonderful it felt to jump into the water or roll around in the snow.

The Farmer Who Loved to Take a Sauna

There is an old Finnish folktale, that demonstrates the Finn's belief in the religious significance of the sauna. It has been around for hundreds of years, and no one really knows who created it. I don't know who to attribute this story to since I've heard variations of this story from many sources, but a version of it appears in the book *"Sweat"* by Mikkel Aaland. It goes something like this:

Once upon a time there was a Finnish farmer who loved to take a sauna. He could tolerate as much heat as any sauna could produce. The hotter the sauna, the happier he was.

Everyone talked about this farmer who could endure more heat than any sauna could provide. Eventually, the Devil himself heard of this farmer and made a special trip all the way from Hell just to meet him.

"I hear you like heat." said the Devil, "I hear that you can take more heat than any sauna can produce."

"Well, I suppose you could say that. The cold makes my old bones ache, and I really do love the heat." replied the farmer modestly.

"I can take you to a place where it is so hot you'll soon be begging for cold." said the Devil.

Excited, the farmer agreed to go with him. As they passed through the gates of Hell, the Devil shouted to his demons to throw more wood on the giant fire.

"More heat! More heat! More heat!" shouted the Devil. "We have a man here who says he loves the heat."

The farmer thanked the Devil for his kindness.

Soon the fires of Hell were so hot that even the tines of the Devil's pitchfork were becoming limp, and the Devil himself was sweating profusely.

"This is wonderful. Can you get it any hotter?" The farmer smiled.

"What? More heat?" the Devil cried. "This fool wants more heat?"

As the Devil glanced about nervously looking for more wood for the fires, all the residents of Hell gathered around the farmer watching him in delighted awe.

Pointing at the Devil, they laughed. "Ha, Ha, Ha, he wants more heat!"

The farmer simply smiled, and once again thanked the Devil for his hospitality.

The Devil was humiliated; the fire of Hell was Heaven for this farmer.

The Devil screamed, "Get out! I never want to see you here again."

So, the farmer returned to his farm. He was sorry to lose the wonderful heat of Hell, but happy to know that his future in Heaven was assured.

Finnish immigrants bring the sauna to America

There was a huge influx of Finnish immigration to North Amercia from the late 1800's to the early 1900's and the first thing they did when they arrived was to build their saunas. They often lived in the sauna while they built their house.

Neighbors who saw the sauna in use were puzzled as to what was going on. Before long, stories began circulating that these strange Finns (who spoke little English and had difficulty explaining themselves) were witches worshipping pagan gods in log temples, and could be seen frolicking around naked in the moonlight.

These misunderstandings finally reached the point where a trial took place in Minnesota in 1880 when a neighbor demanded that their Finnish neighbor's pagan temple be removed. Fortunately, the Finns were able to prove to the judge's satisfaction that the sauna owner was a law abiding Lutheran and that the sauna was a place for cleaning and not for worshipping pagan gods. So the judge ordered the plaintiff to pay the defendant for damage to his reputation as well as to have the sauna moved to a more private location.

Sweden

Like the Finns, the Swedish also loved the sweat bath, which is called Badstuga in Swedish. Some people would take a sweat bath every day, but that was seen as hedonistic and wasteful so it became a tradition that every Saturday evening, when the work of the week was ended, that everyone would take a sweat bath to be fresh and clean in preparation for church on Sunday.

Germany

At its peak the Roman Empire extended beyond the Danube and Rhine rivers in present day Germany, and Roman baths were common. But after the fall of the Roman Empire Europe fell into the Dark Ages and bathing of any sort was considered unhealthy and unnecessary.

It wasn't until the 18th century that sweat bathing was revived in Germany with the interest in health and wellness and the development of spa resorts like the one in the town of Baden-Baden.

In the 20th century German athletes and trainers, impressed by the performance of Finnish athletes, began to include the sauna into their athletic training programs.

In the 1920's and 1930s, Finnish athletes were competing well internationally and claimed that the sauna was a factor in developing their endurance. In particular, the "Flying Finn" Paavo Nurmi, who won nine gold medals in three Olympic competitions, and set 25 track and field world records, attributed much of his success to the sauna.

When German trainers saw the sauna that was built for Finnish athletes during the 1936 Olympics in Berlin, they were quick to adopt it.

Natives of the Pacific Coast

The natives of the Pacific Coast from Alaska to as far south as Northern California used a wooden sweat lodge structure sometimes referred to as a "kashim" as a social and religious center. It was dug partially underground, insulated with dirt or sod with a single tunnel entrance and a small hole in the roof for smoke to escape.

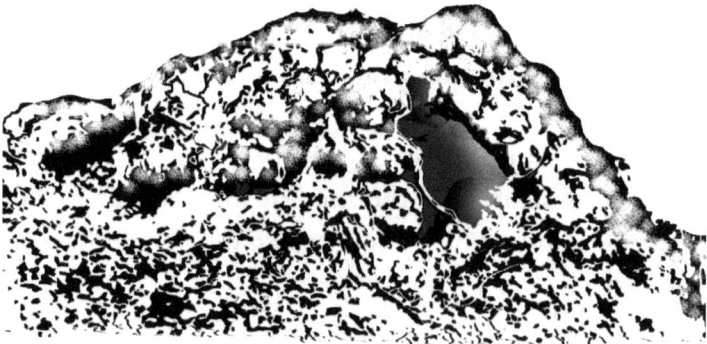

The central Alaskan people did not build wooden sweat lodges like those in the coastal regions because they lacked timber, but they did perform something similar to sweat ceremonies in snow huts (igloos) in the winter, and in animal hide covered tents in the summer months. They burned animal fat to create heat and induce sweating, both for ritual purposes and as a method of treating illness.

The Celts

The Celts were a diverse group of tribal societies in Iron Age Europe (approximately 900 BCE to 100 CE). Their territories ranged from Ireland and Portugal in the west, Scotland in the north, the Black Sea in the east, and northern Italy in the south.

They were polytheistic and worshipped a wide range of gods and goddesses, which they believed could help them with particular problems. In general, the gods were deities of particular skills, such as blacksmithing and warfare, while the goddesses were associated with nature. Iron age carvings of a sun god similar to the illustration below have been discovered.

Ancient stone and sod sweat lodges still exist from this period, and the archeological evidence indicates that the Celts practiced sweat bathing both as a religious ceremony and for healing purposes.

The ancient Greeks

Keeping the male population happy and providing social and recreational facilities was one of the primary duties of ancient Greek rulers. Therefore, public baths were very common in ancient Greek communities.

The Greeks enjoyed a variety of baths, from hot water tubs to hot-air baths. The ancient epic poem the Iliad mentions the Greek man's passion for bathing.

In ancient Greece the baths were a luxury available only to men. Women had few rights and enjoying the public baths was not one of them.

In Greek mythology a Gorgon was a vicious female protective deity. There were three Gorgons, but the one that we are most familiar with is Medusa, who had hair of living, venomous snakes. Carvings of Medusa have been found on ancient Greek bath houses.

The Roman Baths

Roman citizens loved sweat bathing. The early communal baths were called balnum and included steam rooms, dry heat, and hot water. They were so common that there was at least one in every neighborhood.

In 25 BC Emperor Agrippa built the first thermae which was a centrally located pleasure complex, complete with sports halls, restaurants, and various types of sweat rooms and baths. Following Agrippa, Roman Emperors began building grander and more elaborate thermae, with each one trying to out-do his predecessor.

To appease the general population, entrance fees were free or extremely low. All across the social strata from slaves and servants to the very wealthy used these bathhouses. In the mornings guards even brought their prisoners to bathe.

Roman engineers and architects accomplished many amazing feats of engineering associated with the baths. They invented a method to heat the air to temperatures exceeding 210 degrees F. (100 degrees C.) They did this by heating the marble floor, which was raised on pillars, with huge log fires; this hot air was then channeled through earthenware pipes in the walls. The fires were tended continually and the baths were kept continuously hot.

To provide adequate water for washing, pipes large enough to gallop a team of horses through brought running water over long distances. Roman architects designed a vaulted ceiling which, when cast from concrete in one huge section, could span an area large enough to house thousands of bathers.

Roman baths spread throughout the Roman Empire, and depending on the local customs and the time, sometimes men and women bathed together, but other times there were separate facilities.

Roman bathing was a long process, often beginning with vigorous exercise to stimulate the circulation.

Then the bather would proceed through three rooms, going from tepid to hot. The first room, the coolest, was called the "tepidarium". Then the bather would move into the warmer "caldarium", which provided a choice of hot or cold water for washing. The final and hottest chamber was the "laconicum" meaning "brief".

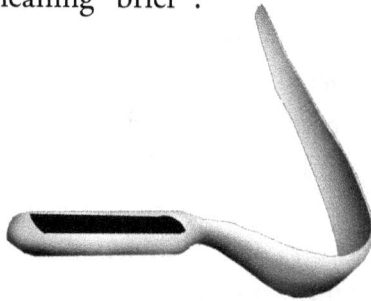

Then it was time for a vigorous massage, which included the scraping off of dead skin with a tool called a "strigil". Which is similar to what we use today when grooming horses.

Next, a dip in the cold pool or "frigidarium" would complete the process.

Afterwards the bather would relax in the outer areas of the thermae where refreshments were available and they would read or converse with friends.

Islam and the Hammam (spreader of warmth)

The word hammam apparently means "spreader of warmth" in Arabic. Conquering Arabs might have encountered Roman and Greek sweat baths in Syria, or Mohammed might have encountered them as a result of his travels as a camel trader. Regardless of how they were discovered, they soon became an important part of Islamic culture.

Until the adoption of the Roman sweat bath concept, Arabs washed only in cold water and never immersed themselves in tubs, which was considered to be bathing in one's own filth.

Mohammed began to recommend sweat baths to his followers around the year 600 CE. As a result of his endorsement of the practice, the Islamic hammam began to proliferate.

Since physical purification is an important part of the Muslim faith the hammam gained religious significance.

The Islamic form of sweat bathing is a five-step process. The first step of the process involves the preparation of the body with heat; the second step involves vigorous massage; the third step involves shaving and removing dead skin; the fourth step is a vigorous soaping; and the process ends with the fifth step, where the bather relaxes and cools off with refreshments while lounging on couches in a rest hall.

Even today, in many parts of the Islamic world, the hammam is a place to socialize and entrance fees are kept low so that everyone can enjoy them. Even the wealthy, who own their own private baths, patronize the public baths to show that they are clean and as reminder that all are equal before Allah.

Since order and cleanliness are essential, an inspector is given the job of ensuring that the baths are clean, and that the water quality is acceptable. The hammam must be open before dawn so that people can bathe before Morning Prayer.

Ginn, the spirit of the Hammam

The Ginn is the spirit who is thought to dwell in the steam, water and darkness of the hammam. The Ginn is not necessarily malicious, but if one encounters the Ginn, Islamic law indicates that you need only say "in the name of Allah" and the Ginn should immediately leave. It is also the practice for the tellak, or bath attendant, to shout before escorting you into the steam room to warn the Ginn of your arrival.

The devil is also thought to use the hamman. It is said that you should not bathe between the last two prayers of the day because that is when the devil and his friends have their baths. They claim that if you happen to find yourself in the hammam with the devil you should begin reciting from the Koran and this will send the devil running away.

Women and the Hammam

When Mohammed first began promoting the use of the hammam, women were forbidden. But as the hygienic benefits became apparent, women were then permitted the use of specific "women only" hammams. It became very popular because it was one of the few opportunities a woman had to socialize with anyone outside the home. Even today, the hamman plays such an important part in the life of many Moslem women, that, in many parts of the world, if a husband prevents his wife from visiting the hammam, she has grounds for divorce.

I have never personally had the opportunity to experience a Hammam, but my oldest daughter enjoyed it while she was working in Turkey. At first she felt a little uncomfortable not really knowing what to expect, and being unaccustomed to having someone else lathering on the soap and massaging her, but she soon began to enjoy it, and loved relaxing afterward in the outer room where the attendants brought out hot apple tea (well it was actually a powdered drink more like warm koolaid) and cookies.

Recommended reading

For a much more in-depth history of sweat bathing around the world I highly recommend the book *"Sweat"* by Mikkel Aaland. This book was published in 1978 by Capra Press and is out of print now, but many libraries and used book stores still have copies of it. Apparently, the author Mikkel Aaland is working on an updated edition.

"There is no death. Only a change of worlds"

Chief Seattle

3

Native American Religious Practices

We fear what we don't understand

The European settlers didn't understand the native culture and what their religious ceremonies represented, and what they didn't understand they feared and tried to eradicate.

Forced conversions to Christianity by missionaries and governments, the banning of religious ceremonies such as the Sweat Lodge, the Sun Dance, and the Potlatch, the banning of the use of traditional languages, the breaking up of families by sending children off to residential schools, the introduction of alcohol, the massacres of entire communities, the deliberate introduction of disease, the list goes on and on. These atrocities were committed partly in an attempt to "civilize" what they perceived to be lazy and backward "savages" but mainly it was done to control them and to steal their traditional lands.

Fortunately, inspite of all these tremendous pressures to give up the Old Ways, enough people were able to retain the teachings and pass them on to us today.

The Great Spirit or Grandfather

The Great Spirit is known by many different names among the many different tribes. For example the concept of the Great Spirit is called Wakan Tanka to the Sioux, and Gitche Manitou to the Cree/Anishinaabi.

The Great Spirit is sometimes compared to the Christian concept of God, except that the Christian God is seen as a separate being, while the Great Spirit is understood to include everything and everyone.

In Harmony with Nature -- We are all Related

Traditionally North American native spiritual belief was an oral tradition passed down from elders to each succeeding generation. It is a nature based belief system that recognizes our need for harmony, balance, and interdependence with Mother Earth and with each other. Like the "three sisters" in a traditional native garden--corn, beans and squash, each puts into the soil what the other needs.

We are no longer in balanced harmony with nature and the result is pollution, climate change, greed, unhappiness and a dependence on chemicals.

Being an oral tradition there are no holy scriptures, and no priests, but rather a series of guidelines based on observations of the natural world. While there are no priests, there are medicine men or women, individuals with highly developed spiritual gifts, who can be called upon for guidance, but each person is responsible for cultivating their own direct connection with Spirit.

Through direct observation of nature it was understood that everything is "alive", that every thing, every rock, plant, animal has a soul, and that we are all related. Science is only now proving what the old timers knew intuitively, that we really are all related, and that our individual well-being relies on the health of the whole.

The Standing People

The Standing People (the trees) were recognized as our brothers and sisters. Trees provide oxygen, and clean the air for all of us to breathe. Their branches are home to the Winged Ones (birds), and give shelter from the heat of the sun, and their roots are home to many smaller creatures.

Before collecting herbs or berries, or before hunting, the plant's or animal's permission would be asked, and thanks would be given in recognition of its sacrifice. Care would be taken not to take more than was needed, and enough of the plants or animals would be left to ensure the continued survival of the species

The Stone People

It is thought that the Stone People (the rocks) contain (or record) all the thoughts, actions and energy that have occurred throughout time in a particular area, and as such are a reservoir of spiritual energy which can be drawn upon when needed.

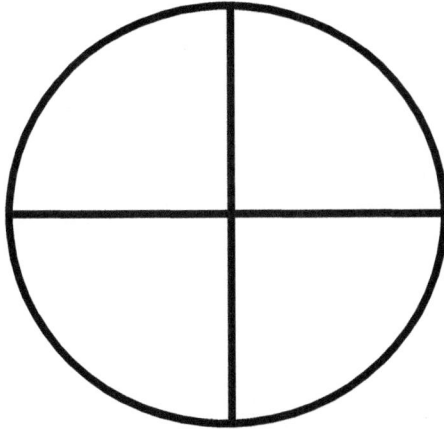

The Significance of the Number Four

The number four is very significant for many reasons:

- There are **four directions** on land
  -- North, South, East and West

- There are **four elements** that make up life
  -- Air, Water, Fire and Earth

- There are **four seasons** of the year
  -- Spring, Summer, Autumn, and Winter

- There are **four races** of mankind
  -- Red, Yellow, Black, and White

- There are **four stages** in a lifetime
  -- Childhood, Youth, Maturity, and Old Age

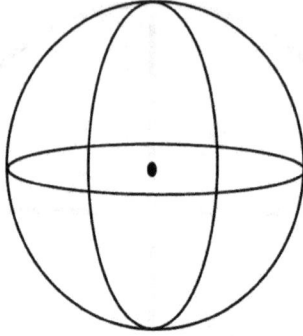

The 7 Sacred Directions

- The **east** is where the sun rises every morning, and signifies a new beginning.

- The **west** is where the sun sets each evening giving us rest for our bodies and our minds.

- The **south** represents warmth and growth. The south also represents harmony, balance, community, and the interdependence of all people and all things

- The **north** is where the cold winds come from which bring us relief from the hot summer weather and gives Mother Earth a chance to rest. The north also represents courage, strength, patience, and endurance.

- **Above** is Father Sky

- **Below** is Mother Earth

- The **center** is within the heart of each individual.

The Circle of Life

The power of the world works in circles. The earth is round, the sun, the moon, and the stars are all round, jagged rocks in a stream eventually wear down and become round from the force of the water, even the wind kicks up circular swirling motions of dust. The sun forms a circle as it rises and falls each day. The seasons form a great circle as they change, always coming back again to where they started. Even the life of a man is a circle from childhood to childhood. There is great power in the center of the circle.

Medicine wheels are circles of stone constructed to focus and direct the energy of the earth and the Stone people for a specific purpose.

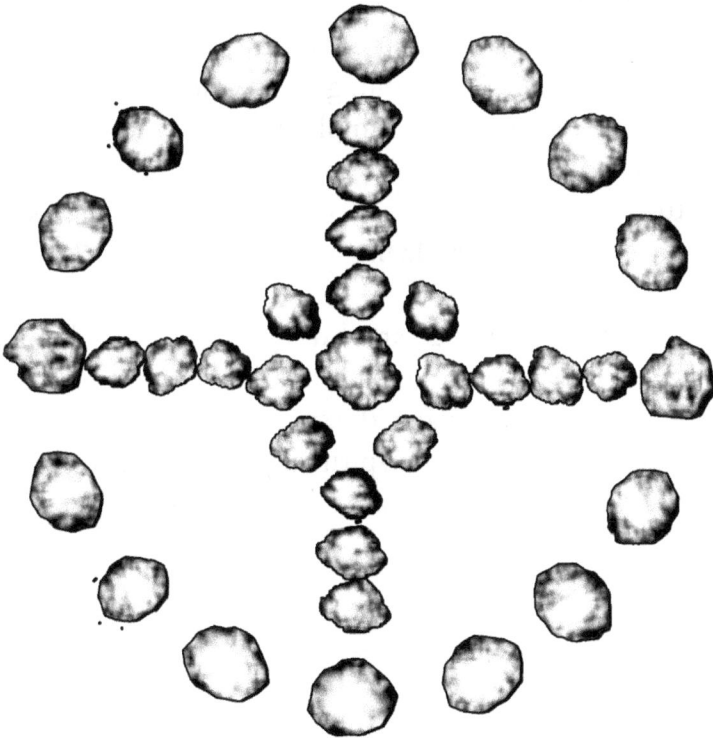

Spiritual beings on a human journey

This world is just a shadow image of the real world. The unseen world of Spirit is the real world, and our time on earth is a sacred spiritual journey, a time of learning,

We are spiritual beings on a human journey. Our bodies are just shells which are part of Mother Earth and return to her when we die, but our spirits are part of the one Great Spirit and when we die our spirit will pass from this world of shadow, darkness, and pain and return to the real world of light.

It is believed that immediately after death the soul lingers around the body for about three days before it moves on to the light of the Great Spirit. Sometimes they are confused and do not realize that they are dead, and sometimes they just need time to complete something before they move on. Some spirits do not move on and simply linger on the earth plane and are felt like a cold chill. Some spirits, after they move on, return to the earth plane as energy to help us, and we can experience this as a warm loving glow.

There are spirits all around us, all the time. Some are here to help us, and some mischievous ones are here to mislead us. Just as on the earth plane, the spirit plane is made up of all sorts, but it is possible for a spiritually perceptive individual, like a shaman or medicine man, to discern the difference.

In balance or out of balance

Traditionally, Native American spirituality does not recognize the concept of hell or the Devil, or evil, everything is simply in balance or out of balance. If one individual has harmed another individual then the situation is seen to be out of balance, punishment does not rectify the situation, rather something, some restitution, must take place to restore the balance.

If a person is not in balance when they die, it is believed that they will be recycled or reincarnated into another body appropriate for their energy, perhaps even a plant or animal, giving them an opportunity to once again die and return to the Great Spirit.

Male and female roles

In the native tradition it was recognized that males and females have their own particular medicine or spiritual power. Neither one being more important than the other, both being equal, both needing the other.

Generally a man was thought to be more adept in the physical world while a woman was thought to be more adept in the hidden or spiritual world. Women were therefore required to bring forth the energy required for the sacred ceremonies that only the men would be required to perform.

Women did not have to take part in purification ceremonies like the sweat lodge because their menstrual cycle was considered to purify them naturally, and their role as mothers kept them rooted to Mother Earth.

But these traditional sex roles were not rigidly fixed so if an individual had traits that were usually considered those of the opposite sex it was considered a blessing from Spirit.

Homosexuality

Homosexuals and transsexuals were considered especially gifted. They were thought to be people who had two souls in one body and could therefore represent both sexes.

Children and Elders

Traditionally, Native American culture had a great respect for the wisdom that comes with age. It was common for children to be raised by the grandparents who, it was recognized, had many lessons to teach the children. If a child had no grandparents other members of the community would take over the grandparent role in rearing the child.

What is considered to be senility in our culture was thought to be a closer connection with Spirit in an elderly native. Being confused simply meant that the person was beginning to spend more and more time with loved ones on the other side.

Children who had what we think of as "imaginary" friends were considered to have the gift of vision or mediumship.

Medicine bundles

A medicine bundle is a collection of objects tied up in a piece of cloth or animal hide. Some medicine bundles might belong to a group of people, and would be passed down from generation to generation, while other medicine bundles would be the private property of the individual. It might contain stones, crystals, feathers, or animal bones.

The individual items in the bundle are talismans or reminders of a particular energy or medicine that the individual or group has or would like to have. The contents of the bundle are sacred and it is inappropriate to ask about or touch another person's medicine bundle. An individual's bundle might be small and worn in a pouch around the neck, or an entire tribe's bundle might be a large item that would be carried around, generation after generation, from place to place, as the group moved.

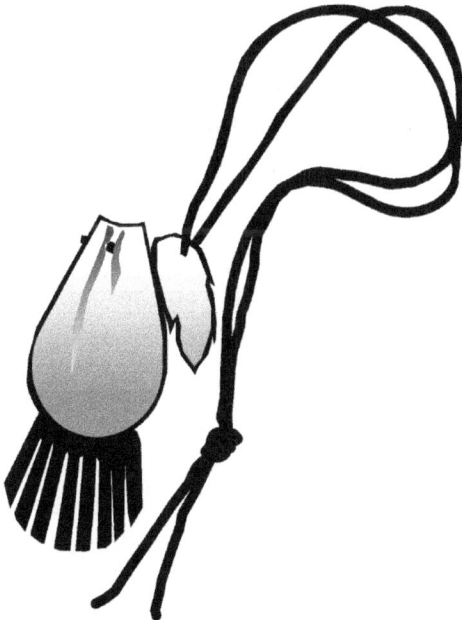

If an individual died without having passed on his medicine bundle it would be burnt so that he would have no ties attaching him to the earth and he would be free to move on.

I witnessed this practice of releasing a deceased individual's ties to the earth plane repeatedly during the time I lived in the isolated community of Sandy Lake in northwestern Ontario back in the early 1980s.

On one occasion a young man had been beaten to death during a fight at a dance (an extremely unusual occurrence on this relatively peaceful alcohol-free reservation at this time). Apparently some alcohol had been smuggled onto the reserve and a bunch of young people got carried away and a fight broke out and one young man was killed.

Once all the investigations were completed the band council decided that the best way for the deceased man, and the community, to move on would be to burn down the building where he was killed. Friends and loved ones brought along some of his belongings, which they included in the fire. A service was held (something of a combination between Christianity and the Old Way) and the young man's spirit was released.

Also, in Sandy Lake it was the custom to never say the name of a recently deceased person in the belief that doing so would inadvertently call them back to the earth plane and prevent them from moving forward. After the one year anniversary of the person's death it was considered "safe" to once again refer to them by name, because by then the individual would be firmly settled in their new life.

The Sacred Pipe

Smoking sacred tobacco in the medicine pipe makes the participant's breath visible. The smoke rising upward is seen as carrying the prayers toward spirit. But it represents far more than just this, the inhalation and exhalation of smoke symbolizes the ebb and flow of all life. The smoke makes our words visible and makes us conscious of what we say while we are smoking the pipe.

The bowl of the pipe symbolizes the female aspect of the Great Spirit -- Mother Earth, while the stem symbolizes the male aspect -- Father Sky, and the bringing together of these two components represents life itself. When not in use the two halves of the pipe are wrapped and carried separately.

Smoking the sacred pipe is an important component of all Native American spiritual ceremonies, signifying the connection between the two planes of existence, the earth plane, and the spirit plane.

A pipe is generally either received as a gift or handmade by its user. An adolescent boy would traditionally receive a pipe as a gift when going on his first Vision Quest, but a woman needed to be beyond menopause before receiving a pipe because the power of her moon cycle (menstrual cycle) was believed to interfere with the medicine of the pipe.

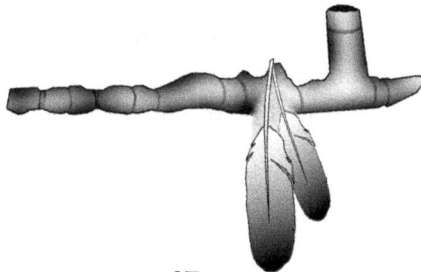

The Pipe Ceremony

There are probably many different rituals involving the use of the pipe, but as with every ceremony, the intention is the most important part.

First, a pinch of tobacco is blessed and "all our relations" (our spirit guides and departed loved ones) are invited to join us as we load the pipe. Once lit, the pipe is offered to the seven directions reminding us that we are one with all creation.

The bowl of the pipe is customarily held in the left hand while the stem is held in the right. The pipe is turned once clockwise before passing it on to the next smoker in a clockwise direction. Many people believe that all of the tobacco in the pipe must be smoked, actually drawn into the body and released, because failing to do so is considered disrespectful to the spirits that we have invited to join us.

I am not certain that actually inhaling the smoke is necessary as long as the smoke is at least drawn into the mouth and then released. It is not that I think the tiny amount of natural tobacco smoke used in a ceremony would be harmful, rather I think that the coughing and gagging of someone unused to smoking would disrupt the solemnity of the occasion.

People who have abused tobacco in the past, but have succeeded in quiting smoking would probably be wiser not to participate in a pipe ceremony. Remember, the magic is not in the tobacco smoke, but in your intention.

The Sundance

The Sundance is a dance of courage and self-sacrifice. It is a time for renewal and purification. The Canadian government banned the ceremony in 1880, and the US government in 1904, ostensibly because they deemed it to be a form of self-torture, but I think it is more likely that it was banned because they feared the power of the dance.

As with many other rituals, only men need to perform the ceremony but it first requires that the women create the sacred circle. A cottonwood tree is cut down and carried to the site and mounted in the middle of the circle symbolically connecting Mother Earth and Father Sky.

Prior to the Sundance the dancers would prepare themselves with a Sweat Lodge Ceremony and three days of fasting.

Undertaking a Sundance is very serious decision. A man who has not danced before must have an experienced sponsor to testify to his worthiness. People struggling with alcohol or drug problems should not dance. The participants dance in the hot sun for four days and four nights to honor the four sacred directions. To quit or to fall is a disgrace and reflects badly on your sponsor and the entire tribe.

Throughout the ceremony the dancers blow eagle bone whistles and drummers pound out a trance inducing rhythmic beat which encourages the dancers and causes them to experience profound visions.

On the fourth day, the flesh of the dancer's chest is

pierced with wooden spikes and a strip of leather is tied from his chest to the Sundance tree in the center of the circle. He then continues to dance until his movements cause the wooden spike to rip through his flesh and free him from the tree.

The purpose of this self-induced suffering is for the man to show his willingness to suffer to protect the entire tribe. Through the piercing he symbolically shares his blood with Mother Earth. Flesh represents ignorance, which confines the spirit, and breaking the skin symbolizes the release of the individual spirit to the Great Spirit.

Women are not required to perform the Sundance because they share their blood with Mother Earth each month during their menstrual cycle, and it is recognized that the suffering they endure during childbirth benefits the entire tribe. A woman in her "moon cycle" (during menstruation) must not enter the Sundance arena, not because she is considered "unclean" as in some other cultures, but rather because she is seen to be too powerful.

The Vision Quest

In some tribes only a person who wanted to become a medicine person or shaman undertook a vision quest. However in other tribes it was undertaken regularly as a means of getting direct guidance from the spirit world. In some tribes it was considered a rite of manhood that every adolescent boy must endure.

Every tribe had different customs regarding the vision quest but generally it involved a purification ritual like the Sweat Lodge Ceremony followed by four days and four nights alone in the wilderness (usually on a hill or mountain), with only a blanket as protection from the elements, and without food or water. Often they would be required to stay within a prescribed circular area. The intention was to stay awake the entire time until the vision came.

Alone and cold, sitting in the dark, focusing on his quest, he faces his deepest fears. The vision, when it comes, is described as being more real than reality. Sometimes it involves an actual one-to-one visit from a human Spirit Guide, other times he might be visited by a Winged One (bird) or Four-Legged or a Crawling One (insect). Often, he would receive a new name and a vision of his future. The message received might be understood instantly, or might require a lifetime to fully understand. Regardless, it is said to be a life changing experience.

The vision quest usually concludes with the quester participating in another purifying Sweat Lodge Ceremony. Then he must publicly display his vision for others in the tribe to see, whether in the form of a song, a dance, or a painting.

The Spirit Calling Ceremony

The Spirit Calling Ceremony or "tying up" ceremony is used to ask for specific help from the Spirit world. Often it is used for healing, for protection, or to find missing persons. These ceremonies are very rare because of the difficulty of finding a medicine person or shaman capable of performing it.

For the ceremony to be successful it is important that every participant come with the right frame of mind. Skepticism and negativity conflict with the positive energy necessary for a successful ceremony.

The ceremony basically involves creating an area or gateway between the two worlds such as a medicine wheel, or a rectangle with stones defining the four directions. An altar is formed from a pile of holy soil upon which is placed an offering of tobacco.

The shaman kneels in front of the altar in the center of the gateway. While the room is smudged with sage and sweet grass an assistant proceeds to tie up the shaman. The shaman is then covered with a blanket and the blanket is again tied up.

Once the shaman is totally immobilized and everything is ready the lights are turned out and the Spirits are called through drumming and chanting. Tiny blue lights sparkling in the darkness are usually the first indications that Spirit has arrived. Conversations can be heard between the shaman and Spirit providing answers to the questions that the ceremony was called to provide. Finally, in a dramatic finale, Spirit unties the shaman and the blanket is thrown off.

Many people are skeptical about this ceremony because they feel there is too much potential for fraud. Certainly it is possible that the shaman might simply be a gifted contortionist and ventriloquist, a con man out to fleece the crowd, but one only has to look closely at the life of the shaman to realize that they are sincere in their desire to work with Spirit and are not really benefiting financially.

As far as I am concerned, the real proof is in whether the information received was accurate or the healing was effective. The Spirit lights, the voices, the ropes falling away and the blanket being thrown off are just little extra touches that remind us that there is far more going on around us than we can possibly see and understand.

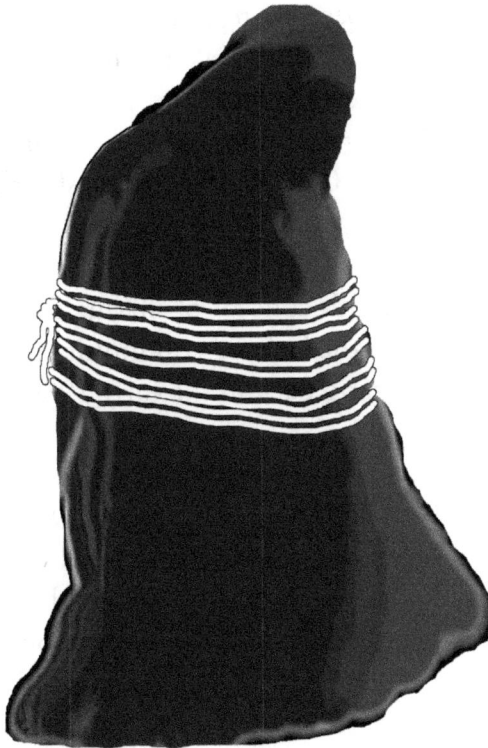

The Potlatch

In the summer months many different tribes such as the Sioux of the Great Plains and the Haida of the Pacific Northwest would gather for what has come to be known as a powwow. It was like a big fair or festival where people would come to trade goods, meet potential spouses, and generally have a good time. There would often be a "Potlatch" or ritual giveaway of gifts. This giveaway was an act of sacrifice, and an individual would often give away everything he owned because, within the native tradition, how well a person was regarded was based on their generosity, not on their ability to hoard goods.

This type of generous behavior worked well within native communities because regardless of how much they gave away they would always be taken care of by others in the community. The concept of sharing, rather than hoarding possessions was foreign to the new white rulers and the Potlatch was banned in Canada in 1885 and shortly thereafter in the United States.

I experienced this concept of sharing first hand many times when I lived in the isolated community of Sandy Lake in northwestern Ontario back in the early 1980s.

There was one incident in particular that when I think back on it now I am disappointed in myself. What happened was that my mother had sent me two small plastic tubs of peanut butter. Food was very expensive and my family of four was living on an unbelievably meager budget. When neighbors came in and saw the unopened tub of peanut butter sitting on my kitchen shelf it was assumed that I would give it to them because what use could I possibly have for a second tub of peanut butter when I already had one. When I was reluctant to give it away my standing in the community was seriously damaged. As the greedy white woman that I am, after that incident, I am a bit ashamed to admit that I began to hide anything that I was not willing to part with.

Recommended reading

I hope that this short introduction has whetted your appetite for what could be a lifetime of study. If you want to learn more about Native American spirituality here are a few books that I strongly recommend to get you started:

"Mother Earth Spirituality" by Ed McGaa

"Thorsons Principles of Native American Spirituality" by Dennis Renault & Timothy Freke

"Black Elk: The Sacred Ways of a Lakota" by Wallace Black Elk & William Lyon.

"Black Elk Speaks" by John G. Neihardt

"It was our belief that the love of possessions is a weakness to be overcome. Its appeal is to the material part, and if allowed its way, it will in time disturb one's spiritual balance. Therefore, children must early learn the beauty of generosity. They are taught to give what they prize most, that they may taste the happiness of giving."

Ohiyesa (Charles Alexander Eastman) Wahpeton Santee Sioux

4

Building the Sweat Lodge

A traditional willow framed sweat lodge is very easy to build. A small group of people with no experience can build one and have it ready for use in a matter of hours using only a few common tools.

Although quick and easy to build, every detail is symbolic. Since the sweat lodge is intended as a doorway to communion with the Creator (or Higher Power if you prefer) and the Spirit world, it is important that you exercise care and respect in everything connected with its construction and its rituals.

What you will need

Building a sweat lodge does not require a lot of equipment. All you really need is a sharp knife, a small pruning saw, a hatchet, a ball of string, a round nosed shovel, and a pitchfork.

You will also need a pail to hold water if your location is near the water's edge, or several pails of water if your site does not have a water source. A metal pail is ideal so that you won't risk melting a hole in it if you get it too close to any hot stones. A metal cup is useful for pouring water on the stones and for offering each participant some water to drink or to pour on their heads.

Remember to bring safe drinking water to keep the participants hydrated throughout the proceedings.

To cover the sweat lodge you will need plastic tarps and plenty of old blankets for insulation and to darken the inside of the lodge. Some clothespins are handy for holding the door blanket closed, but this is not absolutely necessary.

For the ceremony itself you will need something with which to move the hot rocks into the lodge. Traditionally antlers were used, but today it is more common to use a pitchfork. It is possible to simply use a shovel, but this is less desirable because of the likelihood of dragging in some burning coals and causing smoke inside the lodge.

Choosing the right location

Some sweat lodges are intended for one time use only with the site to be returned as closely as possible to its natural state immediately afterward. If you are fortunate enough to have a site that can remain intact for use in future ceremonies particular care must be taken in choosing the placement of the lodge.

Choose a quiet and secluded place where you will have privacy and will not attract attention since you do not want your ceremony to be disturbed by curious onlookers. Finding a site that is isolated enough for privacy and yet easily accessible can be quite a challenge.

Ideally it should be located next to water:

1) For fire safety
2) To enable the participants to cool off afterward with a refreshing swim
3) To invite the participation of the water spirits.

If this is not possible you will have to carry water with you. You will need water to pour on the rocks, extra water in case the fire gets out of control, safe drinking water, and water to cool off overheated participants.

Ask for guidance from the Spirits regarding the best place to build the sweat lodge. Sprinkle pieces of tobacco, or cedar, in the water, and around you on the land, as an offering to show your appreciation for the Spirits' help. Tobacco is one of many sacred gifts available for us to use in our Spiritual activities. Unfortunately, as with many gifts, its misuse has resulted in serious harm to many people, and so some people choose instead to sprinkle cedar needles.

You will get a sense when you have found the right site. Sometimes you will receive a sign or omen indicating that this is the place. Often animals will appear. It is common for beavers or otters to swim up close to shore, or for eagles or other birds to circle overhead. These are very good signs because the animals can sense the positive energy.

Smudging the site

Once the site is selected, a smudging ceremony takes

place to cleanse the area, as well as all of the participants. Burning sage or cedar signifies our intention to make this site holy ground and to remove any negative energy. Any time that we are attempting to make contact with the Spirit world it is important that we invite only the highest and best, and smudging the area reminds us of this intention.

Sage or cedar smoke is believed to remove negativity and draw in positive energy. Light a smudge stick (a bunch of sage, sweet grass, or cedar tied together in a clump) and carry the smoldering twigs around the perimeter of the site, pausing at each of the four directions, north, south, east, and west. Finally, direct some of the smoke over each of the participants.

Some people use a large shell to hold the smoldering twigs, and direct the smoke by fanning a large feather over it. Many Native Americans use eagle feathers to fan the smudge smoke. The eagle is admired because of its great power and speed, and its exceptional vision. Because they can fly so high they are associated with the energy of the sun and are believed to be able to walk between the worlds. Some Native Americans believe that there are spiritual powers that can be obtained by possessing a part of the bird. However, because it is an endangered species protected by US law, it is a felony to possess eagle feathers or claws unless you are a Native American.

The eagle's vision can represent the ability to see the past and the future, and it can also represent seeing new opportunities. As with many other birds they have excellent hearing, which can represent clairaudience (the ability to hear messages from Spirit).

However, it doesn't really matter if you don't have any accessories like shells or feathers, because your intention is what is important. The real magic is in the intention, not in the tools. I have seen people use garbage can lids or metal dustpans to hold the smudge, which might not seem very glamorous but was definitely respectful of Mother Earth by being very careful about preventing fires.

Prayer flags

Next, you can hang up little prayer flags of red, yellow, black and white strips of cloth in the four directions, signifying the four races of mankind, to remind us that we are all related, and as an indication that we are asking the Grandfathers and Grandmothers (our ancestors and Spirit Guides) to come and visit us and help us in the lodge. These prayer flags also serve to mark off the boundaries of the sacred site.

Fire Safety

The decision about where to position the sweat lodge on the site should be based primarily on fire safety. Although there is no rule about which direction the sweat lodge door should face, some people have preferences based on the significance of each of the possible directions, but since fire safety is the primary criterion, choose your fireplace area first. This will determine the direction the sweat lodge door will face since the door opening always faces the fire.

If possible, choose a location for the fire pit close to the water and in a spot that takes advantage of natural windbreaks. Fire is a gift from the Creator. If handled carefully and tended with respect, fire is a blessing, but if treated carelessly, fire can be destructive. Make fire safety a primary consideration when setting up your sweat lodge.

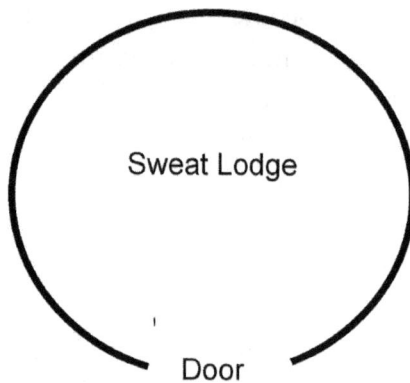

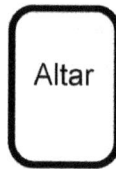

Sweat Lodge

Door

Altar

Fire Pit

As you can see from the diagram, the fire pit, the altar, and the sweat lodge form a straight line with the fire pit at one end, the altar in the center and the lodge at the other end of the line.

Which way should the door face?

If there is no obvious choice of where to place the fire pit then you can choose based on what direction you want the door opening to face. As we discussed in Chapter 3 there are 7 Sacred Directions, and four possible directions where your door opening into the lodge can be facing. Here are some suggestions:

The east is where the sun rises every morning, and signifies a new beginning. By facing your door to the east you might be indicating that you want a new beginning in your life. Usually when we perform the sweat lodge ceremony we are asking Spirit for help with some new beginning in our lives, like help with our relationships, guidance regarding our careers, or freedom from an addiction. For this reason, people often choose to have their door face east.

The west is where the sun sets each evening and facing your door in this direction might represent that we recognize that we need rest for our bodies and our minds, in other words, indicating our recognition that dependence on the Creator gives us freedom from worry.

The south represents warmth and growth. You might choose to have the door of a winter sweat lodge facing south in anticipation of the warm summer sun that will soon be returning, or it could be indicating that you are asking for growth in some endeavor like expanding your business. The south also represents harmony, balance, community, and the interdependence of all people and all things

The north is where the cold winds come from which bring us relief from the hot summer weather and gives Mother Earth a chance to rest. Perhaps facing your door in this direction could indicate your concern for the state of the environment, and the abuse that Mother Earth has been suffering as a result of man's greed and arrogance.

The north also refers to certain mental or emotional aspects of a person's life--courage, strength, patience, and endurance. If your intention in enduring the hardships of the sweat lodge is to develop courage and strength through exhibiting patience and endurance then you might consider pointing the door to the north.

Gathering the materials

Prayers and offerings are given prior to gathering the stones, firewood and willow and before beginning the actual construction of the fire pit, the altar, and the lodge. The materials will probably need to be gathered a short distance from the actual sweat lodge site. When you arrive at the spot where the materials are to be gathered say a prayer of thanks and sprinkle an offering of tobacco or cedar.

If you have enough people on hand to help, the sweat lodge can be ready in 3 to 4 hours. If there are only a couple of people it will probably take all day.

Every aspect of the job of gathering the materials

and building the sweat lodge is important and must be undertaken with the proper attitude of respect. As with all Spiritual endeavors, intention is everything. In the case of the sweat lodge, people usually fast while building the lodge as a reminder to keep their intention focused and pure. However, fasting doesn't have to mean going without water. In this case it is a good idea to drink plenty of water and stay well hydrated throughout the day. You will be losing a lot of water through sweating, and dehydration can cause serious health problems.

Remember, the sweat lodge ceremony is not an endurance test. There are no extra "spiritual" bonus marks for suffering. The fasting is just a gentle reminder to keep your intention focused and pure. If you find that being hungry makes it more difficult for you to maintain the right attitude then go ahead and eat something. Maybe next time you will find that you are better able to maintain the proper attitude while fasting.

It takes a couple of hours and a lot of firewood to heat the rocks properly, but if you have enough people to help, you can start the fire early in the building process, and the rocks will be hot by the time the lodge is finished. Remember that once the fire is started one person needs to be responsible for watching the fire, staying with it, and continually stocking it with firewood and watching for sparks.

The fire pit

Ideally your fire would be situated on bedrock with good natural protection from the wind, far enough from any overhanging tree branches, and close to the waters edge.

However, if you don't have such an idyllic site then to be safe you should dig a pit about 3 feet by 4 feet and at least 2 feet deep. Build a windbreak of rocks around the pit, higher on the side of the prevailing wind.

Stack at least two layers of dry firewood on the bottom of the fire pit to form a base for the rocks. These bottom layers will eventually become the coals that will heat the rocks, but don't put the rocks in yet, get the fire going well first. On top of these layers of firewood place pine cones, pine needles, dried grasses, and other dry kindling materials. Create a tipi or cone shape of dry small sticks, no larger in diameter than your thumb, on top of the pile of firewood and kindling.

Say "thank you" to the wood as you place it in position, and smudge it before starting the fire.

I find that using one or two scrunched up pieces of newspaper inside the cone of kindling helps to get the fire started, but many people feel that using other materials to start the fire is not appropriate, that nothing other than wood, tobacco or a special offering should be placed in this ceremonial fire. However, I feel that using a few pieces of newspaper is an acceptable tool, similar to using matches, but you should go with your own feelings concerning what is appropriate.

The idea is to get a good fire going using the smaller sticks and branches and gradually build up a bed of coals upon which to place the stones. With a good fire on top the larger pieces of wood underneath will gradually begin to burn and this is what really heats up the stones. As this kindling starts to catch fire keep stocking more small pieces of wood on top, once the fire is burning well, and there are some good hot coals, begin placing the stones in the fire, and keep topping it off with more firewood.

What kind of wood should you use?

Ideally, it would be good to use natural wood which was gathered from the forest floor without cutting down live trees or breaking off their branches, but this is not always possible, especially in damp areas, so wood in other forms is also acceptable. Never use pressure-treated wood (the ashes from pressure-treated would are poisonous), used lumber with nails in it, or rotted wood (it does not burn well and would be disrespectful).

A mixture of hardwood and softwood is ideal, since the hardwood burns longer, but the softwood is easier to get started burning. Cedar is ideal since it burns very easily and is regarded by many as a spiritually imbued wood whose special properties can enhance the ceremony. Cedar shavings are sometimes used as kindling and add fragrance to the fire. Evergreen needles are sometimes used in this manner as well. Experiment with the different combinations of wood that is available in your area, since each type of wood imparts a different energy and heat, but don't get too hung up on this. Remember that the magic is in the intention, not in the tools you use.

Remember to keep at least 4 buckets of water around in case something happens and the fire gets out of control.

Collecting the stones

The stones you choose should be small round boulders about the size of cantaloupes, and definitely no larger than a child's head. Smaller ones are lighter and easier to manipulate when moving them from the fire pit to the sweat lodge, but you don't want them so small that they fall through the tines of the pitchfork or antlers. They should be gathered from dry fields, hillsides or mountainsides. Limestone, granite, or volcanic lava rocks are preferred. Do not use sandstone or other stones with obvious cracks where water can be trapped because stones with trapped moisture or those taken from streams or near wet places can explode when heated.

Many people choose to use 28 stones. Seven stones are brought into the lodge during each of the 4 prayer sessions, or "endurances" (see the significance of the number four in Chapter 3). Using 7 stones is in recognition of the 7 Sacred Directions.

It might be a good idea to collect a few extra in case one or two crack in the fire. If you are fortunate enough to have a permanent location for your sweat lodge it is a good idea to keep a few extra piles of rocks close by so that you can perform sweat lodge ceremonies in the winter, when there is snow on the ground and suitable rocks are difficult to collect.

Thank the stones as they are being collected and smudge them when you have piled them up at the lodge site.

Collecting the willow for the sweat lodge frame

The sweat lodge frame is usually made of willow, but any flexible sapling that grows in abundance in your area will do.

Willow is a wonderful gift from the Creator. It grows very rapidly in clusters, and cutting one or two poles from a cluster does not hurt the tree, in fact it simply encourages further sprouting. It is very flexible, it bends easily without breaking, and yet when tied together they make a very strong framework.

Willow bark contains salicin, which is a painkiller and the effective ingredient in aspirin. It is also a blood thinner and is used extensively for the prevention of heart attacks. A very versatile plant, there are many other ailments for which willow and aspirin are effective, and many other products that can be made from willow. In a healing sweat lodge ceremony some people choose to put willow in the water in order to benefit from its healing properties.

Willow usually grows in slightly wet areas, so it is not a good idea to gather the stones in the same area as you gather the willow. Select young willow saplings that are about an inch in diameter or slightly less. Don't get ones that are too thick because they will be more difficult to cut and bend. It is amazing how strong these thin flexible saplings become when they are tied together. Something for us to contemplate while we collect the willow.

A willow's life cycle reflects the natural cycle of all life. In the fall, the leaves of the willow die and return to the earth, but in the spring, new leaves come out. The willow reminds us that we are all part of this cycle of life and will one day return to the real world, the eternal world of the Creator. The sweat lodge reminds us of this true life to come.

Use a small pruning saw to cut the saplings. Chain saws are unnecessary, noisy and dangerous when working in clumps of willow. Willow is a soft wood and is easy to cut with a pruning saw or even a knife. The physical labor of cutting it is an important part of the preparation ritual for the sweat lodge. When harvesting the poles, offer tobacco, cedar or sage to the spirit of the willows and thank them for giving their lives for the Sweat lodge and also for providing their healing powers. Cut only one or two saplings out of every small clump. Do not leave the area an unsightly mess, and do not damage the surrounding growth unnecessarily. Respect for Mother Earth is one of the primary lessons of the sweat lodge.

How many willow saplings will you need?

The number of poles required to build the lodge varies depending on the finished size. You will need one upright pole for every 2 feet of circumference. For those of you who cannot remember your elementary school geometry, the formula for determining the circumference of a circle is:

Circumference = 3.14 X Diameter

Therefore, if you are planning to build a sweat lodge that is 11 feet across it will measure about 34 ½ feet around and you will need 18 vertical poles (round it up to an even number so that each pole will have a partner on the other side to be tied to).

You will also need poles to form the horizontal supports. These ones can be the same thickness or thinner than the vertical poles. For these supports you will need approximately 3 times the circumference of the lodge in length, in this case about 103 feet (about 11 - 10 foot long poles).

If all this seems too complicated simply cut some saplings and bring them back to the sweat lodge site and keep going back for more until you have enough.

Carry the cut saplings back to the lodge site, and remove the branches and leaves. Save the soft branches and leaves for the floor of the Lodge, to give participants a clean place to sit. The floor of the sweat lodge can become wet and muddy with all the steam and sweat, so having the soft leaves and delicate branches to sit on is very pleasant. Some people bring along a small square of carpet or canvas, or a towel to sit on.

You do not have to peel the bark off the saplings, but some people peel strips of bark to use instead of string to tie the lodge together. This is quite a bit of extra work but many people feel that it looks and feels better than one tied with string.

Building the sweat lodge frame

Dig a circular pit about 3 feet in diameter in the spot that will be the center of the sweat lodge. This is the pit where the heated stones will be placed, and it is sometimes called the "Hand of the Creator". This pit does not have to be very deep, usually only about 8 inches deep so that it is deep enough to contain the hot stones (to keep them from rolling onto the participants) and keep the water that is poured on the rocks contained. It is most important that the top grass and organic matter is removed so that it does not start smoldering when the heated rocks are placed in it.

The soil from this circular pit is used to build a small altar mound in front of the lodge entrance, five or six feet away from the door of the sweat lodge, between the seat lodge and the fire pit. On this altar, participants can place the items that they want to use during the ceremony, such as drums or pipes or other personally significant items as well as items like jewelry and glasses that participants do not want to take inside.

A sweat lodge that has an 11-foot diameter will seat eight to ten people. It is usually designed very low so that you have to crawl on your hands and knees into the lodge. This is intended to remind us that we are going back into the womb of Mother Earth. A slightly taller lodge is easier to get in and out of, something to consider if you have participants who have difficulty crawling through a low opening. However, keep in mind that a taller lodge is harder to heat. Heat rises, so the hottest spot in the lodge is closest to the top. 4 feet tall at the center works well. At this height it heats up well, and you still have to crawl in on your hands and knees, but will allow a large man to sit comfortably without having to slouch.

To lay out the exact position of the lodge place a stick with a 5 1/2 foot long piece of string tied to it in the center of the stone pit. Use this string like a compass to measure where the outer poles of the lodge will be positioned. Use a stick to draw the circumference on the ground.

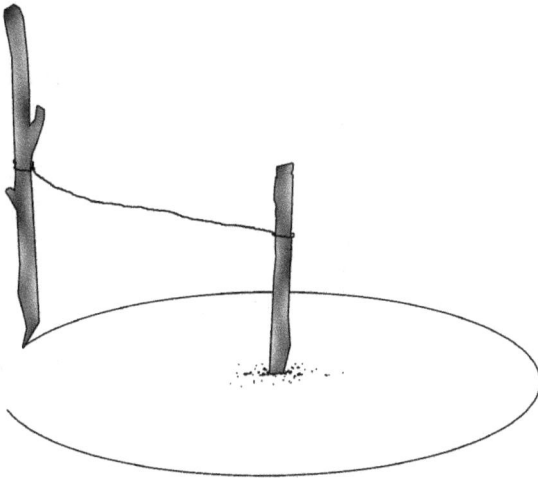

Drawing a Circle

Cut the thickest end of the vertical sapling poles with your knife to form a point to make it easier to push them into the ground. You might find it easier to use a heavier pointed stick to make the holes. Be sure the sharpened saplings are embedded deeply enough into the ground (8 to 10 inches deep) so they hold firmly when they are bent over and tied together to form the frame. If the ground is very hard and you are having trouble getting the sharpened saplings into the ground, an alternative method is to cut some thicker stakes about 2 feet long that you can hammer into the ground with the flat edge of your hatchet and then tie the flexible saplings to these stakes.

You will be pushing the sharpened ends into the ground about every 2 feet around the circumference, leaving a slightly wider opening for the doorway. Start by locating the door and place one pointed end into the ground on either side of where the door opening will be. Then place another one into the ground on the opposite side of the sweat lodge.

Carefully bend the sapling over to meet and overlap

its partner on the other side, making sure that they form the height that you want and tie them together with string or willow bark which you have peeled in long strips.

Once all the vertical poles are tied together you are ready to proceed with placing the 4 horizontal supporting rings in place. Start on one side of the door opening about 6 inches to a foot from the ground and tie a sapling to each of the upright pieces, overlapping the ends when you need to add a new piece. Work your way around the lodge till you reach the other side of the door opening. Then do the same thing all around about a foot higher up. Add two more supporting rings until the 4th level is completed at the top.

The sweat lodge frame is now complete and you can place the willow leaves or other grass, cedar, or sage on the floor for people to sit on, but leave an open path from the doorway to the rock pit so that the rocks can be rolled or carried by pitchfork into the lodge.

Any leftover willow should be piled neatly off to the side, out of the way to be burnt after the ceremony.

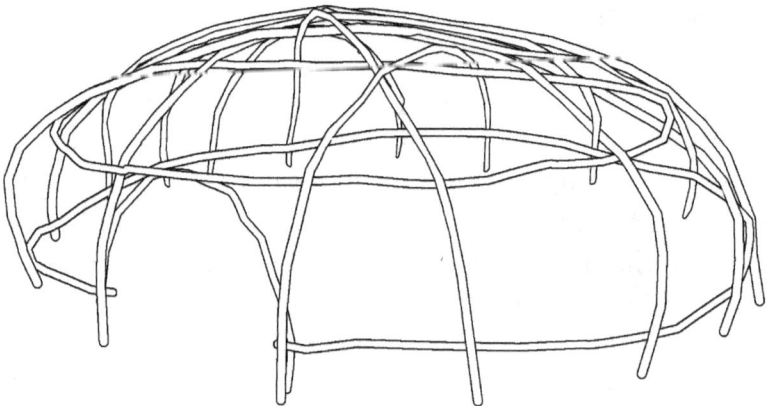

Covering the sweat lodge

In the past, buffalo hides covered the frame, but now we use plastic tarps and blankets. Tarps are ideal for covering the sweat lodge frame, they are impermeable so they make an excellent windbreak, they are opaque so they help darken the lodge, they are waterproof so they will not be affected by the condensing steam, and they usually have reinforced holes in the corners that make it easy to tie them to the lodge frame. Thick plastic sheeting like the kind that is used for vapor barriers in house construction will also work.

I prefer to first cover the frame with a layer of tarps (or thick plastic sheeting) and then cover the tarps with blankets. Putting the waterproof layer first prevents the blankets from getting too wet from the condensing steam, but it does result in the condensation dripping down inside the lodge so some people prefer to use a layer of blankets first, but then you are stuck dragging home a pile of damp blankets. Try it both ways and decide which way you prefer.

The tarps should lay on the ground about 6 inches and be held down with rocks or wood to prevent drafts or light from getting in at ground level. To hold the blankets in place use twine to tie the corner of each blanket to the corner of a blanket draped on the opposite side of the lodge.

The blankets provide heat and sound insulation and also help to block out all the light. The more blankets you use, the better the insulation and the darker the lodge will be. The goal is to have total darkness inside the lodge when the door is closed.

For the door, use a couple of thick blankets wider than the door opening which can be folded back to act as a hinge.

That is all there is to the construction of a sweat lodge. Once the rocks are heated you are ready to begin the sweat lodge ceremony.

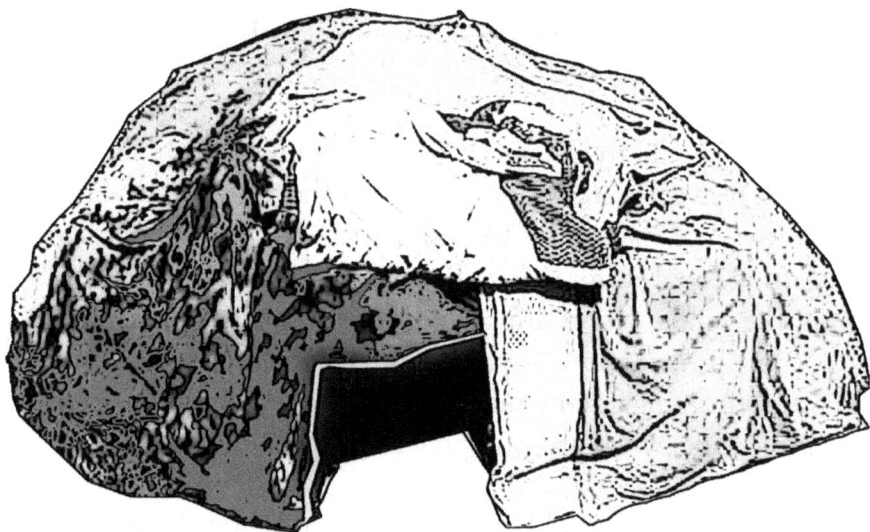

5

The Sweat Lodge Ceremony

What to expect?

What can you expect if you have the privilege of participating in a traditional Lakota style Sweat Lodge Ceremony? First of all, it is important to remember that by participating in a sweat lodge ceremony you are consciously and deliberately opening yourself up to the Spirit world. Therefore, the sweat lodge demands sincerity and respect. Your sincerity and good intention in participating in the sweat lodge will result in your having a positive experience.

According to traditional Native beliefs there are varying degrees of more or less evolved energies around us all the time. I intentionally do not refer to these energies as good and bad, because I believe that everything works together for our benefit, even things that seem bad at the time.

One of the principles of the religion of Spiritualism, which I adhere to, is that we are all evolving, whether in this life or after the transition to the next life. I believe that it is not really necessary to be frightened of lower energies (or demons as some religions describe them) because we only attract to ourselves energies that are in harmony with our own energy.

There are many variations on the sweat lodge ceremony. What I am describing here is a typical Lakota style hot rock sweat lodge ceremony. Inipi is the Lakota Sioux term for this type of sweat lodge. However, I do not think that any one way is better than another, and if you happen to be participating in a sweat lodge that doesn't exactly follow the pattern that I am describing just remember to be open-minded and respectful.

When should you take part in a sweat lodge?

The sweat lodge is primarily a purification ceremony. It is often performed prior to other ceremonies. People take part in sweat lodges for many reasons; to ask for help and guidance from Spirit, for healing, and as a means of balancing their lives. Some people choose to participate in a sweat lodge after experiencing disturbing events as a way of ridding themselves of negative energy.

I have never heard of a person's health being harmed as a result of participating in a sweat lodge ceremony, however, to be on the safe side, if you have any concerns in this regard it would be a good idea to discuss it with your doctor prior to participating.

The most important thing is to listen to your body. The sweat lodge is not intended to be an endurance test. Yes there is some discomfort involved, but in reality this discomfort is more mental then physical. If you find yourself experiencing severe physical discomfort there is no shame in asking for the door to be opened so that you can get out.

How often you choose to participate in a sweat lodge is entirely up to you. Some people choose to do it annually, or on special occasions, and I've heard of other people who do it on a daily basis. While I believe the sweat lodge to be a gift to us from the Creator, and is a tremendous benefit both spiritually and physically, I can't imagine being able to find the time in my busy life to perform a full sweat lodge ceremony that often, so do it as often as you are reasonably able.

Should a woman participate during her "moon" time?

Women traditionally did not participate in sweat lodges during their "moon" time (while menstruating), not because they are considered unclean, but rather because they are thought to be too powerful. I personally do not think that there is any physical reason why a woman should be excluded, but in consideration of other participants who might believe that a menstruating woman's power will interfere with their own connection with spirit, it is probably better not to. Unless, of course, it is a special women's "moon" lodge. Besides, menstruation is believed to be purifying for women so the endurances of the sweat lodge are thought to be unnecessary.

Physical and spiritual preparation

Many people abstain from eating food the day of the sweat lodge in order to focus their mind, and to make it easier to tolerate the heat. But it is important that you be well hydrated, so drink plenty of water, and NO coffee, tea or alcohol immediately before (since they have a dehydrating effect).

The primary spiritual preparation is simply to set your intention, in other words decide why you are taking part in this sweat lodge, be consciously aware of what you are hoping to achieve, and ideally spend a little time in meditation beforehand.

What do you wear?

While attitudes toward nudity are relaxed in Finland and other Scandinavian countries, and to sweat bath there clothed is unheard of, in my experience native people tend to be very modest so it would be very unusual to find a mixed group (males and females) participating in a sweat lodge naked.

The best thing to do is ask your host what you should wear, but generally it is appropriate for a man to wear a bathing suit (loose style not a Speedo type) and a T-shirt. Women should wear either a long skirt and a T-shirt or possibly a long loose T-shirt over a bathing suit. Constricting clothing is not recommended since it tends to cut off circulation and inhibit sweating.

Even if you are participating in a sweat lodge where it is acceptable to be naked you will be sweating a lot and will probably find that you will be more comfortable in a big loose T-shirt. Remember to bring a change of clothes and a plastic bag because you will definitely want to change out of these sweaty clothes afterward.

Bring a towel to sit on, and an extra one to dry off with especially if there will be an opportunity to swim afterwards.

The actual ceremony

Usually there will be two leaders, *'the one who pours the water'* (the person who guides the activities inside the lodge), and *'the stone tender'* (the one who stays outside watching the fire, opening and closing the lodge door, and tending to the stones).

These two leaders will begin the ceremony by smudging the area, usually with a mixture of sage and sweet grass. Smudging involves lighting the sage and sweet grass on some sort of fireproof surface and walking around directing the smoke, either with your hand or a feather, all around the sacred area.

Sage is believed to have been the second gift from the Creator. It is associated with wisdom and provides protection from negative energies, which is why it is usually burnt before beginning any ceremony.

Sweetgrass is a long reed-like plant that grows in marshy areas. Its sweet aroma attracts positive energy. The smudging is usually done in a clockwise circle around the entire lodge area, including the fire pit, the altar, and sweat lodge itself. The participants then line up and the smudge smoke is directed at them.

Entering the lodge

One by one the participants walk to the altar and leave any items that they do not want to bring with them into the sweat lodge. People often leave their medicine pouches, their jewelry, and even their wallets. It is inappropriate to touch anyone else's belongings when they are on the altar. It is usually suggested that you remove all jewelry before entering the sweat lodge, both for symbolic reasons (in recognition of the fact that we were born with nothing and we will not take anything with us when we cross over into spirit) and for practical reasons (it gets really hot inside the sweat lodge and metal jewelry can burn you) but personally the only jewelry I wear is my wedding ring and I prefer not to take it off.

It is customary to bring in drums, rattles, or flutes that you might want to use during the singing and chanting, but keep in mind that it will become very humid inside the sweat lodge and this can cause leather drums to loosen up and go flat. It strikes me as very odd to bring a synthetic drum into the sweat lodge, but it certainly improves the sound of the drumming to use a drum that is impervious to water.

The "one who pours the water" will place an offering of tobacco on the altar. Tobacco is one of the most sacred plants. It is believed to have been the first gift from the Creator. Used reverently as it was intended, this herb brings clarity and can transform negative energies into positive energies. The smoke of burning tobacco is like a telephone line to the Spirit world. It is so powerful that it plays a role in almost every ritual, ceremony, or healing. It has calming properties, which is why it was traditionally used in the peace pipe during band council meetings.

One by one the participants crawl through the doorway and into the lodge. The first person in goes to left and crawls in a clockwise manner right around the central stone pit and sits to the right of the door opening. The one who pours the water is usually the last one in and sits to the left of the door opening. This organized manner of entering the sweat lodge replicates the circle of life, and the power of the circle.

Some people choose to bring in small pieces of cloth, called prayer twists, which they tie to the willow frame of the sweat lodge above their head.

Some people like to perform a pipe ceremony at the beginning of the sweat lodge before the stones are brought in, other people leave the pipe out on the altar and the stone tender hands it in at the end so that the pipe ceremony can be performed after the fourth session. But not every sweat lodge ceremony includes a pipe ceremony.

The stone tender passes in the pail of water, the scoop, the leader's drum, and pouches of tobacco, sage, sweetgrass, and cedar. Some people choose to put a few willow leaves in the water that will be poured on the rocks because this is thought to promote healing.

The Stone People enter the lodge

The stone tender brings 7 stones (the stone people) and places them in the pit in the center of the lodge. This pit is a very holy spot that is sometimes referred to as the *'hand of the Creator'*. Antlers were traditionally used to move the stones, but today most people use a pitchfork. A shovel will work, however with a shovel it is more difficult to pick up only the stone. If the stone tender inadvertently brings some of the wood or hot coals into the lodge the resulting smoke makes it difficult to breathe.

As each stone is brought inside, the participants

welcome the stone people by saying **"Hello Grandfathers, we are glad that you are here"** which shows that we acknowledge that we are related to them as we are with all creation, and then an offering of tobacco and cedar is sprinkled on the rocks. Cedar is believed to have been the third gift from the Creator. This tree grows all over the world and has many uses, and when a small amount is sprinkled on the hot stones the fragrant smoke purifies the air inside the lodge.

Note: I do not speak the Sioux language so I think it would be inappropriate of me to attempt the Sioux phrases, prayers, responses that are often used in sweat lodges. Instead of risking mangling the language, I will simply attempt to give the English equivalents that I am familiar with, besides, the actual words themselves are not important, what is important is that we understand what we are saying and that we are sincere in our requests.

At this point *'the one who pours the water'* opens the sweat lodge ceremony with a prayer, thanking *"the Stone People"* and *"the Standing People"* for their participation, acknowledging our own human frailty, inviting 'all our relations' to join us in the sweat lodge, and petitioning for assistance from the spirit world.

At this point the leader pours water on each of the seven stones causing steam to rise up from them heating the sweat lodge. These seven stones represent the seven sacred directions, which comprise everything in the universe.

The first stone is dedicated to the Great Spirit, who is the center of everything, the next stone is dedicated to Mother Earth, then to 'all our relations' (this refers to all living things as well as the spirits of our loved ones who have passed on), then one for each direction of the earth, north, south, east, and west.

The Seven Sacred Directions - everything in perfect balance

The East is the direction where the sun rises every morning, bringing new life and a chance to start our lives over. The sun rising in the east reminds us that we cannot go back, but we can go forward and let go of any of the previous day's perceived failures and start over again. Were you kind enough, patient enough, loving enough yesterday? Perhaps not, but today you have the wonderful opportunity to start again.

The South represents warmth. The sun comes to warm and energize us. It balances the cold winds from the north. We love the warmth and the sunshine, but the warm South winds reminds us that we need everything in moderation, too much of even a good thing can hurt us.

The West is where the sun goes down to allow us to sleep, to rest our bodies and our minds. Scientists have recently proven what we all knew instinctively, that our bodies' natural rhythm is to sleep at night and work in the daytime. It is hard on our bodies to have to work the night shift.

The North is where the cold winds come from to bring us relief from the hot summer. As our bodies' need a time to rest, so does Mother Earth.

Above is the home of the Creator and where the Eagle flies. Above reminds us that there is far more to life than what we can see, touch, or feel. Just because we human beings cannot see or prove something yet, does not mean that it does not exist. From above and all around us comes our Spiritual energy and this is where our prayers are answered.

Below is our Mother Earth, the planet that is our home, she deserves our love, respect, and protection for without her there is no life, she gives us everything we need to live.

Inside us is where our spiritual energy or our soul lives. Our bodies are a gift from the Creator and a home for our spirit or soul while we journey through this life. Our bodies are wonderful vehicles to teach us lessons about humility, suffering, and kindness and therefore deserve our love and respect.

Into the darkness

The door is closed, and the inside of the sweat lodge becomes pitch black, hot, and steamy. Why does the ceremony take place in darkness? Some people say that it is because we as humans would not be able to understand the visible sight of spirits that come into the lodge during a ceremony. Perhaps, but it also has the effect of focusing our attention inward once visual distractions are gone, and causes us to face our most primal fears.

Do you remember your fear of the darkness, lying in bed at night as a child, how every sound seemed magnified and threatening? Something similar happens to many otherwise rational people when the sweat lodge door flap closes. It is at this point that some first-timers panic and decide that the sweat lodge experience is not for them. At any point in the ceremony you can call out and ask to leave the lodge. It is not an endurance test. However, if you can overcome this initial fear you will find that the experience is definitely worth it.

I think that another reason for the darkness is that since the interior of the sweat lodge represents the womb of Mother Earth, its darkness represents human ignorance, the recognition that while we are tied to these human bodies we are unable to see the reality of what is actually going on around us, but that this is okay because eventually we know that we will come out of this darkness.

As your eyes become accustomed to the dark you will notice the red glow of the stone people and faces and other images might begin to appear to you. Sometimes little lights began to flicker in the darkness indicating that the Spirit people have arrived. Depending on what we are ready for, and the purpose of the sweat lodge, other phenomena may also take place.

The four "endurances"

There are four sessions (often referred to as "endurances") in the typical sweat lodge. This is in recognition of the significance of the number four: the four directions on land, the four elements that make up life, the four seasons of the year, the four races of mankind, and the four stages in a lifetime.

Each session lasts anywhere from 15 minutes to an hour of guided prayer, individual prayers, chanting and drumming. I have heard of sweat lodges being held in total silence, but I have never participated in one of these. I imagine that there would be different lessons to learn in such a sweat lodge.

In the sweat ceremony, a talking stick is sometimes passed so that everyone will have an opportunity to speak and to listen. Sometimes these are elaborately carved sticks, but they don't have to be, it can be as simple as a twig of willow or a cedar branch. Since willow and cedar are sacred plants it is believed that the speaker speaks more clearly when holding it.

Chanting

We often sing in the lodge. I find that singing and drumming focuses my attention and draws it away from the physical discomfort, as such it helps clear away any obstructions to clarity.

One of my favorite song/chants goes like this:

Oh, Great Spirit, of earth and sky and sea
You are inside, and all around me

Drumming, the heartbeat of Mother Earth

For me, drumming is a vitally important part of the sweat lodge ceremony. The rhythmic, repetitive drumbeats are a wonderful way of focusing our attention, and it brings everyone in the lodge in sync together.

When the beat of the drum takes over, all feelings of discomfort fade into the distance, and your entire body begins to pulse in time with the beat. Everything seems to pulse, the ground you are sitting on, the lodge frame itself, and the air around you. It is as if you are really feeling the heartbeat of Mother Earth.

It is relatively common during drumming sessions, whether inside the sweat lodge or out in a drumming meditation, for people to have "out of body" experiences, the sensation of floating up and out of your body and being able to look down and see yourself and even to travel long distances and view places and events that our logical minds tell us is impossible. Drumming seems to facilitate the opening of the doorway to the other world.

The temperature inside the sweat lodge

The temperature in the sweat lodge is regulated by how much water is put on the rocks. More water results in a hotter lodge but then it cools down faster because the water causes the rocks to loose their heat faster.

At the end of each session the door flap is opened for a breath of fresh air. Sometimes drinking water is passed around to the participants. We give thanks for the water since it is one of the basic elements for our survival, and to show our respect, water is first given Mother Earth to drink before we partake ourselves.

If you need to leave sweat lodge, the best time to leave is when the door flap is open between sessions, this way you will not disturb the prayers and chanting of the other participants. Otherwise, it is not customary to leave the sweat lodge between rounds.

When we are ready the stone tender brings in 7 more stones for the next session. Once again all the rocks are lightly sprinkled with tobacco and cedar as they are put into the center pit with the original seven stones.

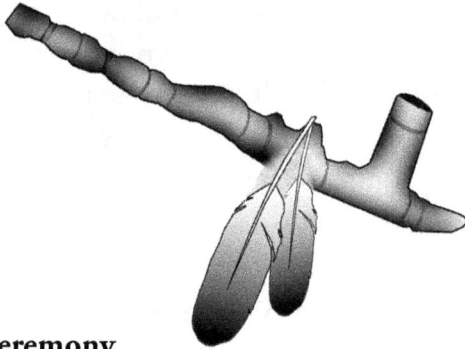

The Pipe Ceremony

Sometimes, immediately after the four endurances of the sweat lodge ceremony, a pipe ceremony takes place, but this is not absolutely necessary. In fact, for those who have abused tobacco in the past it might be better not to participate.

The pipe ceremony symbolizes truth. The placing of tobacco in a sacred pipe symbolizes the entire universe. When it is lit it represents the fire of life, and when it is smoked, the universe passes through the smoker's body and is sent back to the Great Spirit, reminding us that we are one with everything and everyone else in the universe.

The tobacco smoke makes our words visible, reminding us to be conscious of what we say, both while smoking the pipe, and afterward in our daily lives.

Congratulations, you made it!

After the fourth session the leader will call for the door flap to be opened and the participants will crawl back out into the cool air. It is usually best to sit quietly or lie down, drink some water, and give yourself a bit of a rest before you stand up.

It is wonderful in the summer months if you are able to take a swim afterward. It is so refreshing, and you are then able to change into your clean dry clothes. After a winter sweat being out the snow feels great, but be careful to quickly towel off and change into your warm dry clothes so that you don't get a chill.

But we are not quite finished yet. Now it is time for the cleanup. The blankets and tarps have to be removed from the sweat lodge frame and folded. Any leftover willow pieces and any willow leaves from the floor of the lodge need to be burnt in the fire. If the sweat lodge is not to be used in the future, it must be reverently disassembled and burnt, and this site returned as closely as possible to its original state.

Someone needs to stay with the fire until it has completely burnt down, until the coals have actually burnt away. For fire safety, it is not enough to simply put the fire out with water, even when it appears to have gone out it can start up again. Besides, half burnt coals are unsightly and make it more difficult to start the fire next time. So instead of making this a chore for one person, this is a good time to crack open the picnic baskets, pull out the lawn chairs, and enjoy it.

In conclusion

The sweat lodge ceremony is intended to be healing and spiritual, not a test of how much heat you can endure. Don't worry if the ceremony differs slightly from what I've described. Just remember to be respectful of the sweat leader, and the other participants. Keep in mind that the magic is in your intent and sincerity, not in how formally you adhere to a specific ritual.

The sweat lodge ceremony is easy to describe, but impossible to really understand until you have experienced it for yourself. Each time is different, each experience is different, and the lessons we learn are exactly what we need at the moment.

Additional reading

There are not very many books currently in print regarding the sweat lodge, but a couple that I can suggest are:

"The Lakota Ritual of the Sweat Lodge" by Raymond A. Bucko

"The Native American Sweat Lodge: History and Legends" by Joseph Bruchac

Totem Animals

6

One of the primary lessons of the sweat lodge, and the theme of this book, is that we are related to every other living thing, and can learn from every living thing.

Often, during the sweat lodge ceremony or afterwards, participants experience an encounter with, or a vision of, an animal. Sometimes these experiences take place in our mind, and some people downplay the experience, claiming that it is simply a delusion resulting from the heat or some sort of group hypnosis. But just because something takes place in our mind does not mean that it is not "real".

If you would like guidance from a totem animal, make that your intention when participating in the sweat lodge ceremony. Simply ask your totem animal to come to you. The characteristics of the animal that comes to you during your meditation will either reflect traits that you need to develop or traits that you need to control.

We are not expected to believe that these images and totems are gods or beings of great intelligence The qualities and characteristics of each animal represent an archetypal power that can help us to learn more about ourselves and the invisible world of spirit.

Medicine power

The word "totem" simply means medicine power or qualities. Not medicine in our western medical sense of "swallow this liquid and your sore throat will disappear", but medicine in the sense of guidance to help us live a better life. These totem animals that come to us in our meditations or our dreams have something to teach us.

Any kind of animal can be a totem animal. Some people get hung up on expecting that their totem animal will be something that they consider sexy or powerful like an eagle or a wolf and are disappointed when an ant or a mouse shows up. But actually, no animal medicine is stronger or more powerful than another. The totem animal that shows up for you is the one that you can most benefit from at this point in your life. Some totem animals stay with you throughout your entire life and tend to reflect something about your basic personality, while other animals will come to you to help you overcome a particular problem.

Closely observe the animal that comes to you. What is it doing? Ask yourself, "how does this apply in my life", and "what is this animal trying to teach me".

Learn as much as possible about the characteristics of your totem animal. The more you understand about your totem animal's individual characteristics and behaviors, the more you will understand about your own abilities. When you begin to recognize these abilities and then use them in your everyday life, you will find that you become more adept at handling life's challenges.

The predator/prey relationship

One important aspect for you to study is the predator and prey relationship. If your totem animal is a predator you should study the characteristics of its prey. For example, if the owl is your totem then you should also study the mouse. If your totem animal is the prey, then study its predator. Both predator and prey have qualities that will be beneficial for you to understand. Both can teach you things that you can apply to your life circumstances.

When ancient priests and medicine men wanted to invoke the energy of a particular animal they would mimic the animal by dressing themselves in animal skins, imitating its posture, movement and sound dancing, and singing the animal's call. By performing this ritual they honored the totem animal, and released the archetypical energies behind it into their lives. It is not necessary for us to cover ourselves in animal skins to perform this same ritual. Dancing, strutting around and making animal sounds in the privacy of our own home can release these same archetypical energies into our lives

Augers

Augers are people who have the ability to converse with animals. To develop this valuable skill the first thing you must do is believe that you can do it. Make it your intention, then ask the animal world for help. Expose yourself to the natural world by spending time meditating outdoors, being in the presence of animals both wild and domesticated. Look for small things that catch your attention, ask yourself what this means, and pay attention to the words and images that suddenly pop into your mind.

I certainly don't claim to be proficient at this but there have been times when animals have clearly spoken to me. I remember one experience in particular that took place on a visit to the Shedd Aquarium in Chicago. I was standing alone in front of an enormous tank of fish, thinking about how beautiful and graceful they looked, when one of the fish stopped directly in front of my face and looked me straight in the eye. I definitely got the impression it was a female.

She said, "Yes, many of us are very pretty, but more than that, we think and feel, even those of us that are not so pretty."

The experience was awe-inspiring. I was shocked and immediately felt tremendous guilt. Up until that point I had enjoyed fishing. After this experience, the "sport" no longer appealed me. Perhaps I sound like a hypocrite since I am not a vegetarian, I still eat fish and meat, and I have gone fishing on a few occasions since. But I can no longer justify torturing fish as a "sport" for my entertainment.

Talismans, amulets and fetishes

A fetish is a sacred object thought to have magical qualities or spiritual powers. They are found in every religion. In Catholicism there is the Rosary and the Crucifix, and in Eastern Orthodox religion icons or pictures of saints play a prominent role, while Tibetan Buddhist's use prayer bracelets and flags.

Talismans or amulets are good luck charms that are "charged" through some ritual or meditative act. Eagle claws and feathers are examples of talismans. The power of the talisman is not in the object itself, but in our focus on it. They have a suggestive effect on the mind.

Talismans are not limited to just a few "backward" tribes. Virtually every culture and religion uses them. A few examples of talismans that are common in our society include the St. Christopher medal that so many people hang in their car, the crucifix they wear around their neck, and the many relics of saints that people cherish.

Any item that helps you focus on a spiritual ritual can be a talisman.

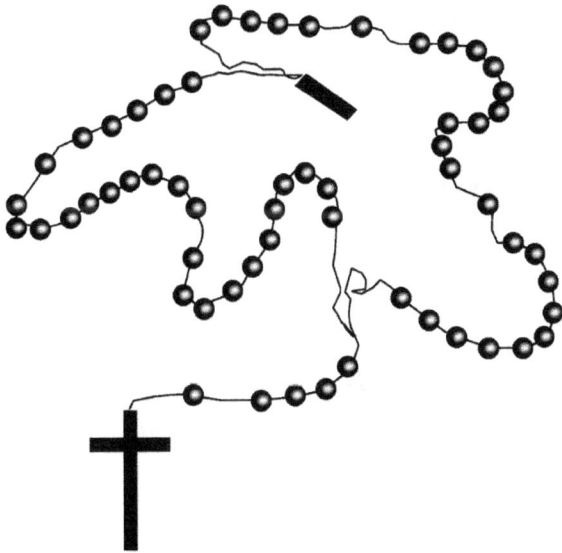

Some common totem animal characteristics

The following are my thoughts and opinions about some of the more common North American totem animals. Just because someone says that a particular animal or a color represents a specific thing does not mean that this is necessarily true for everyone. When a totem animal comes to you, ask for its help in interpreting what it is telling you. Remember that you alone have the answer inside.

Mammals

Bat -- The bat is not a bird but a flying mammal. It symbolizes change and transformation. Hanging upside down it represents looking at things from a different perspective. Although they can symbolize fear and darkness, bats are wonderfully proficient in the use of their many different senses, their eyesight which is specifically adapted to low light, plus sonar in their noses and excellent hearing give them the ability to move around in darkness.

Bear -- Many Native people consider bears to be close relatives to humans because of their ability to walk on 2 feet. Anyone who has ever seen a bear being skinned will recognize another reason for the close connection, a bear carcass without its fur looks startlingly like a human being.

The Black Bear tends to be a solitary creature who, unless spoiled through human foolishness, will avoid contact with people. (Actually their color can range anywhere from black to golden brown, but they are referred to as the Black Bear to differentiate them from their far more fierce cousin the Grizzly, or Brown Bear.) Although extremely strong they are not aggressive, unless they feel that they, or their cubs, are threatened. They might appear fat and ungainly, but in fact they are fast runners, excellent climbers and swimmers. Their ability to hibernate in the winter shows us that we can go within for all the resources we need for survival.

Beaver -- Beavers spend most of their time in the water only venturing on shore to cut down trees and brush to eat and to build their dams with. Water is associated with dreams and emotions. What is the beaver trying to teach you about your emotions?

The beavers' teeth continue to grow throughout their life and they must chew continually in order to keep them worn down. This continual chewing symbolizes the need for continual action.

Beavers are master builders; able to build dams so strong that it often requires dynamite to break them up. I remember being on a mining tour in Cobalt in Northern Ontario and as the bus took us from one location to the next the tour guide pointed out a beaver dam close to the road. He explained that there had been an ongoing battle between those beavers and local humans for several years. Every spring the beaver dam would cause the water to rise and flood the highway, and every year government employees would have to break up the damn.

Each time they broke it down within a few weeks the dam was back looking exactly like the one they had broken up. One of the workers decided to try an experiment. He spray-painted some letters on the exposed top of the dam. Then they blew up the damn. As usual, within a few weeks the dam was back, and this time, to their amazement, the spray-painted letters were once again visible. It appeared that the beavers had rebuilt the dam exactly the way it had been previously, and except for wood that had been too badly damaged in the explosion, they had reused much of the original wood, almost as though they were working from blueprints.

I get so frustrated when I encounter beaver dams when on a canoe trip, but I must admit that I admire their industriousness and determination, traits that I would like more of in my life.

Buffalo -- The buffalo represents abundance. At one time

the herds of buffalo roaming across North America were so large that they numbered in the millions and for an entire herd to run past could take more than a day. The meat and hide of the buffalo was vitally important to the survival of the Plains Indians. In the 1870s the US and Canadian governments deliberately killed off most of the buffalo herds in an attempt to starve the native people into submission.

The buffalo reminds us that it is not necessary to struggle to survive. The hump on its back is symbolic of reserves of energy. A reminder that it is not necessary to push or force, simply to follow the easiest path.

Wildcats such as **Bobcat, Panther, Cougar, Lynx** -- These solitary nighttime hunters, are known for their stealth, silence, and good eyesight. They are able to see what others try to hide. These wildcats are associated with mysticism, secrets and sexual magic.

Coyote -- In many native traditions coyote is a trickster like the Raven. They are playful and love to have fun. They are very intelligent and renowned for their ability to adapt to new situations. A cooperative hunter, they will work together as a group to take down prey. Family oriented, they often mate for life, with the male taking care of the pregnant female and helping to care for the young.

Deer, Caribou, Elk -- These animals epitomize gentleness and innocence. Their antlers remind us of antenna, symbolizing attunement to spirit. Deer, in particular, are said to possess "love medicine" and have the power to attract the opposite sex or to heal broken hearts.

Fast and silent, their fawn color is perfect camouflage; with their tails down they seem to just disappear into the trees.

Fox -- The Fox is best known for its adaptability and cunning. The key to their success in surviving in a rapidly disappearing woodland environment is adaptability. They are seldom seen and seem to camouflage themselves. They are most visible at dawn and dusk, the time when the two worlds intersect. In this way they represent shape shifting, invisibility, and magic.

They have very keen hearing, vision, and sense of smell. These traits symbolize clairaudience, clairvoyance, and clairgustance. They are a mass of contradictions. They are monogamous and tend to have one partner throughout their life but are solitary half of the year. They are part of the dog family but have many cat characteristics. They can be charming and playful and use this quality to beguile their prey before they strike.

Groundhog, Woodchuck, Gopher, Prairie Dog

-- Considered pests by farmers and ranchers, these sociable creatures live in communities of underground burrows with tunnels connecting numerous rooms. They make sure that they always have alternate exits.

To create these tunnels they kick the dirt out behind them as they dig. Many native people consider these little piles of dirt to be holy because they represent purity, an animal doing what the Creator designed it to do. They are sociable and affectionate toward each other. They are surprisingly clean. They maintain separate toilet rooms within their burrows and they even bury their own excrement. They hibernate part of the year and this is associated with dreamtime, shamanistic trances, and altered states of consciousness.

Moose -- The Moose is a series of contradictions. I've heard it said that the Moose looks as though a committee designed it. It appears ungainly but is actually very fast and nimble. It can sound like a freight train running through the forest knocking over trees, but can also move silently and deftly avoid obstructions.

It is a huge powerful animal and yet it is not a predator, its primary diet is water plants. It is associated with feminine energies such as creativity and intuition, because it spends so much time in the water. The Moose as a totem can represent mediumship or the ability to go between worlds. The Moose has few predators with the exception of the grizzly bear.

Mouse -- The mouse totem reminds us that bigger is not necessarily better. Mouse medicine represents attention to detail. Almost all predators feed on mice, so they compensate for this by having three or four litters a year.

Opossum -- The only marsupial in North America, their young are born in a pouch on the abdomen.

They tend to be nocturnal, and have the most amazing ability to play dead as a means of self-defense. They are able to go into a self-induced state of shock in which their heart rate slows, their breathing slows, and they appear to be dead. They even give off a scent of death that momentarily confuses their attacker and gives them an opportunity to escape. The opossum represents false fronts and deception.

Otter -- This water mammal represents joy, playfulness and sharing. They love to play and have a great sense of humor. You seldom see an otter alone, they are very sociable and are usually found in groups of two or three.

On one canoe trip in Northern Ontario my husband and I noticed a lone otter about 20 or 30 feet away from us on the right side of the canoe. He was bobbing around, chattering away, seeming to enjoy performing for an audience. He had our undivided attention. Just then we heard a huge splash immediately beside the left side of the canoe. Startled, I screamed, and almost dropped my paddle. It was then that I realized that it was just another otter that had silently come up right beside the canoe while our attention was focused on his buddy. I swear that the two otters were laughing at the joke they played on us. We could still hear them laughing as we continued on our way.

On another canoe trip we were camped one night in a very isolated spot many miles from the nearest road. During the night we were awakened by sounds of splashing and squealing. We got up quietly and witnessed three young otters sliding down the muddy riverbank into the water. They took turns scampering up the hill and then sliding down laughing and squealing just like children on a slide at a water park.

Porcupine -- These calm, gentle animals shuffle along at their own pace. They never seem to be in a hurry probably because few predators want to come near their sharp quills. It is a myth that porcupines shoot their quills. The quills are loosely attached and when threatened the porcupine has the ability to make them stand out from his body and any attacker attempting to bite the porcupine will get a mouthful. The porcupine can also swing its hind end and short tail towards its attacker causing the quills to connect with his opponent. The quills are hollow and have a barb on the end and when they go in the barb expands and works its way further in. It is very difficult to get out, and very painful.

Most animals know better than to tangle with a porcupine. However, years ago we had a dog that never seemed to learn its lesson. It had several painful encounters requiring expensive visits to the veterinarian, and even when the vet thought she had gotten them all, a few months would go by and another quill, which had worked its way right through the dog's flesh, would pop out the other side.

Rabbit -- Rabbits are fast and nimble, they travel by leaps and hops. Could this represent rapid changes taking place in your life? They have lots of predators so to compensate they have lots of babies.

Raccoon -- Raccoons are known for their curiosity, dexterity, and adaptability. These nocturnal animals seem to be able to survive anywhere from the most isolated wilderness to the biggest city. Running around at night with the distinctive mask around their eyes they symbolize mystery. They usually try to avoid human contact, and will not attack but if cornered they can be ferocious and have very sharp claws.

As a child I remember my father engaging in an ongoing battle to keep raccoons out of our garbage. Every day he would try something new to thwart them. Heavy stones, elaborately knotted ropes, he tried everything and I think the raccoons enjoyed the challenge because every morning we would get up and find the garbage cans open and the garbage strewn around. It was incredible. Finally my father gave up and began putting the garbage in the trunk of the car and taking it to work with him everyday.

Rat -- Many people are disturbed at the thought of having a rat as a totem animal, but rats represent success, shrewdness, abundance and adaptability. Who would not want more of those traits?

Skunk -- Because of its smell, many people are initially disturbed at the thought of having a skunk as a totem animal. But the skunk is a wonderful totem, since, because of its smell, it does not have to get out of the way of any animal; it is self-assured, confident, and silent. The skunk symbolizes respect and self-esteem.

Squirrel -- Squirrels symbolize activity and preparedness. If a squirrel totem comes to you could it be that you are afraid of not having enough, or are they reminding you to stock up for winter?

Weasel -- Weasels can squeeze through very narrow spaces. They have an excellent sense of smell. They represent silent observation, slyness and pursuit.

Wolf -- These misunderstood predators are fast, strong, intelligent and have a keen sense of smell and hearing. Wolves have a carefully defined social structure, there is usually an alpha male and an alpha female, and everyone in the pack knows their place. The wolf represents a balance between authority and democracy. The entire pack helps care for the young.

Birds

Although we recognize that we are related to every living thing, many Native people believe that we are more closely related to birds because we share the ability to walk on 2 feet.

Birds symbolize the soul and the soul's ability to soar free of the earth, they represent the union of the conscious and unconscious. Throughout history many cultures have viewed them as deities or gods who move easily between heaven and earth.

We, as earthbound humans, have always envied birds their ability to fly. Birds fly by flapping their wings or by taking advantage of natural air currents that allow them to soar and glide seemingly effortlessly. I think that one of the lessons they teach us is that there is a time to flap and a time to glide, a time to work and a time to let things happen naturally. Just like us when we are beginning a new task, takeoff and landing are the most difficult parts. At first we have to work hard, flap our wings a bit, but then, if we can find the upward currents, we get some momentum going and it gets easier and we are often able to just glide.

Many birds migrate with the change of seasons in search of food sources and a more pleasant climate. I can really relate to this, every year when I see the geese heading south I am ready to go with them. Although it does not appeal to everyone, following the sun just feels right for me. The amazing thing about migrating birds is that they seem to be born with the knowledge of the route, they don't have a map to follow, but by following their inner guidance they seldom get lost. I think that as humans we tend to get off track when we stop listening to our own inner guidance system.

Some birds adapt to their surroundings as the seasons change instead of migrating. We can compare this to people who prefer to experience the four seasons.

Most birds have excellent vision and can see clearly over long distances. This is symbolic of developing intuition or clairvoyance, of being able to see the future. Perhaps, if a bird comes to you as your totem animal, it might mean that they are there to help you develop your intuition.

For birds, feathers serve three purposes: 1) They are hollow and therefore very light. This helps birds fly by providing lift without weight. 2) Feathers trap pockets of air that provide the bird with insulation to keep it warm. 3) Feathers form an outer coat that helps protect the bird from injury.

For us, feathers are a reminder of the qualities, or medicine, that we are endeavoring to work on in ourselves. Perhaps their light weight can remind us to "lighten up" and take things less seriously, and their insulating and protective qualities can remind us that we are always protected.

Birds often leave us a gift of their feathers. We can use these feathers that the birds have given us as part of our spiritual rituals. They can be used to sweep away energy debris and otherwise cleanse the aura with feathers. They are often used in smudging to spread the purifying smoke around a person or an area.

Some Common North American Birds

Blue Jay -- Blue represents the throat chakra, and is a reminder to never be afraid to speak out what you know to be the truth. These birds might seem to be bullies, noisy and argumentative, but Blue Jays are also fearless and can work together as a team to drive off predators. These traits can symbolize to us the importance of the proper use of our power. As with all birds, Blue Jays represent the connection between heaven and earth, but in the case of the blue Jay, it can indicate dabbling or playing in both worlds but not being serious about either.

Cardinal -- Red is a color that represents passion and the base chakra. Their bright red color reminds us to go ahead and stand out in the crowd. Their loud call reminds us to make ourselves heard, to live our passion.

Chickadee -- Sometimes called the bird of truth. These small fearless birds with a black cap and a cheery call are very, sociable, cooperative and travel in groups.

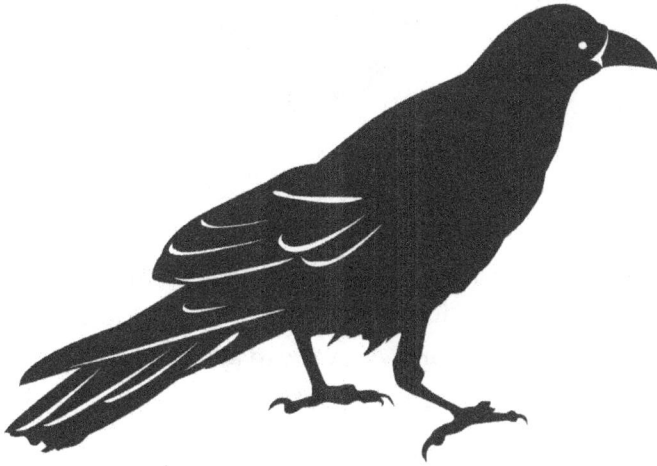

Crow or the Raven -- These two birds are from the same family but the Raven is quite a bit larger. They are often considered the smartest of all birds. They can outwit other birds and animals, and even humans.

They are the messengers of the gods. The Norse god Odin had a pair of ravens as messengers. Black is the color of creation and mystery.

Crows and ravens do not sing as such, except for males when they are courting, but they have an actual language that we can learn if we take the time. They use their language to warn other birds and other animals of danger. They can mimic other birds' calls, and can even be taught to speak our language. They are cooperative and watchful and join together to fight off owls. They use tools to help them crack nuts and seeds.

Duck -- Affectionate and community-oriented water birds. Water is a primal life source. Totems associated with water symbolize the mysteries of the subconscious and unconscious mind as well as emotions. A river can symbolize the passing of time.

Eagle -- The eagle is admired because of its great power and speed, and its exceptional vision. Because they can fly so high they are associated with the energy of the sun and are believed to be able to walk between the worlds. Some Native Americans believe that there are spiritual powers that can be obtained by possessing a part of the bird. However,

because it is an endangered species protected by US law, it is a felony to possess eagle feathers or claws unless you are a Native American.

The eagle's vision can represent the ability to see the past and the future, and it can also represent seeing new opportunities. As with many other birds they have excellent hearing, which can represent clairaudience.

Eagles also represent sexual energy. Their dramatic ritual of mating in the sky involves flying far up into the sky then coming together to copulate as they hurtle downward separating just before they hit the ground.

Geese -- These birds represent loyalty and teamwork. They usually mate for life. Canada geese migrate every year searching out new opportunities. As they fly in a V formation they are constantly shifting formation to create favorable wind drafts for those behind them, their constant honking is like yelling out encouragement to the others. If one is too weak to fly, others will stay behind with it until it either dies or becomes strong enough to continue and catch up with the main flock.

Pheasant -- Some people consider pheasants to be the stupidest of birds. It's true that you can practically trip over them on the ground, and hunting pheasants is so easy it shouldn't be considered a sport. But these beautiful birds have at least one strong point; they are masters of the art of diversion. Walking through the bush you often come upon them on the ground creating a scene, dancing, and drumming their wings, distracting predators away from their young.

Hawk -- Like the eagle the Hawk is a bird of prey. With its strength and keen eyesight, the Hawk represents leadership, deliberation, and foresight.

Heron -- The Heron is a water bird, a wader, standing silently, patiently with its long legs in the marshes ready to catch a fish in its beak. The Heron can represent patience and timing.

Hummingbird -- Fast and fearless, these tiny little birds symbolize accomplishing what is seemingly impossible. They have a very fast metabolism and can perform feats that other birds cannot. For example, they can actually fly backward, and they can hibernate overnight to conserve energy. Incredibly, they can migrate up to 2500 miles.

The Hummingbird is considered to be a healing bird and can heal both long-standing illnesses and problems in relationships.

Loon -- Loons are awkward on land but extremely graceful in the water. Excellent swimmers, they can dive down and swim underwater for more than five minutes without surfacing. They run across the water to get enough momentum to take off, and when they do manage to get into the air their flapping is very noisy.

The call of the Loon is one of the most wonderful sounds of the wild, eerie, and mysterious. The Loon is associated with the moon and inspires creativity.

Owl -- The owl is mistakenly feared by some as the "bringer of death". Owl medicine is very powerful for discerning the truth in a situation, but its use should not be taken lightly.

The owl is the symbol of the night, fertility, seduction, magic, darkness, wisdom, prophecy, clairvoyance, and spirit contact. They have outstanding vision and hearing and can locate prey by sound. Their ability to fly silently allows them to sneak up on their prey. Their poor sense of smell makes them one of the few predators of the skunk.

They seem to have a sixth sense that gives them the ability to be in the right place at the right time. They are hunting even when they appear to be just sitting and relaxing, in reality they are watching and listening and waiting for the right opportunity.

Robin -- Their red breast color represents the base chakra, passion, and Kundalini energy. Their appearance after a long winter is a welcome sign of spring. They are very vocal, and males fight by singing at each other. Excellent parents, they can raise more than one brood each season, forcing the previous brood out of the nest when it is time for them to move out on their own. Could this be a lesson for overprotective human parents?

Vulture -- This misunderstood bird is usually associated with death and decay, but actually represents purification and harmony. Its scavenging helps keep the environment clean and germ-free.

They have keen eyesight and an excellent sense of smell. Once they get into the "zone" they can soar on the air currents for hours without flapping their wings. This ability to soar effortlessly away from the earth (or the mundane, the physical) into the sky (the spiritual) is something that we all aspire to.

Woodpecker -- To me the woodpecker represents drumming, beating out the heartbeat of mother Earth, repetition, and nourishing ourselves through our own efforts.

Insects

The insect world reminds us that bigger is not always better. The metamorphosis that many insects experience, from one stage of life to another, reminds us that change is inevitable.

Ant -- Ants represent order, discipline and community activity. If an ant comes to you as a totem animal, it would be wise for you to spend some time watching the industrious activity of an anthill and reflect about what message they have for you.

Bee -- Bees represent fertility, productivity, and the sweetness/honey of life. Other than the aggressive African "killer" bees, our North American honey bees are generally docile insects with a job to do and will seldom sting unless provoked.

Butterfly -- Butterflies represent transformation, metamorphosis, lightness and joy. The transformation from caterpillar to butterfly is very dramatic. Like the butterfly, we experience many transitions in our lives, but the most dramatic is the transition that takes place when we discard our physical bodies and pass over into the spirit world.

Dragonfly -- The hunter predator of flying insects. I love the fact that dragonflies eat mosquitoes. Dragonflies inhabit two realms, water and air, which represent the emotional and mental. During the first part of their lives they live in the water as nymphs until they grow wings and become the dragonflies that we recognize. They need the warmth and energy of the sun, just as we need the warmth and energy of spirit. Their many colors are reflections of the colors of light.

Frog -- Frogs are amphibians, four-legged vertebrates that live on both land and in water, and which, over their life cycle, transform from egg to tadpole to frog. Frogs are associated with lunar energy, water/emotions, sensitivity, abundance, and fertility. Since the external temperature controls their body heat, they need the energy of the sun to stay warm.

Spider -- The spider represents creativity, building and rebuilding, and is sometimes referred to as "the keeper of knowledge". All spiders are poisonous but generally not to humans, their venom is used to immobilize their prey.

Many cultures have a Grandmother Spider myth, similar to the Greek myth of how Prometheus stole fire from the gods and delivered it to humans. In the Grandmother Spider story it was a water spider that carried a spark from a fire on her back to bring the gift of fire to the world.

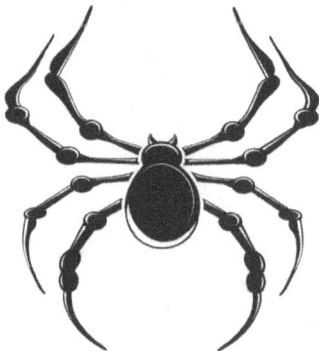

Reptiles

Snake -- Snakes are usually associated with death and rebirth because of their ability to shed their skin. They represent transformation, healing, wisdom, and the awakening of creative forces. Most snakes avoid confrontation, but when they strike they strike fast. Their jaws unhinge to allow them to swallow larger prey. What does this characteristic represent to you?

Turtle -- Turtles live their lives in and around water. They represent longevity and the primal mother, and remind us that Mother Earth provides all of our needs. Turtles lay their eggs on shore and the newly hatched babies experience their first challenge as they struggle to get to the water. Like humans, they are omnivorous and opportunistic. Many of the natives of North America referred to what we now call North America as "Turtle Island".

Recommended reading:

For a much more in-depth discussion of animals and spirituality I highly recommend the book "***Animal Speak: The Spiritual and Magical Powers of Creatures Great and Small***" written by Ted Andrews and published by Llewellyn. The ISBN is 0-87542-028-1.

The Sweat Lodge & Health

7

There have been very few cases of a person being harmed as a result of participating in a sweat lodge ceremony. In fact, throughout history the sweat lodge was considered to be a very effective form of medical treatment. However, if you are on any medication, or have any serious illness or heart, circulatory, or respiratory problems you should discuss it with your doctor prior to participating.

The most important thing is to listen to your body. The sweat lodge is not intended to be an endurance test. Yes, there is some discomfort involved, but in reality this discomfort is more mental then physical. If you find yourself experiencing severe physical discomfort there is no shame in asking for the door to be opened so that you can get out.

Tips to ensure a safe sweat lodge experience:

• Drink plenty of water, before, during, and after the sweat lodge to keep you hydrated. Avoid coffee, tea, and alcohol because they are dehydrating.

• Eating a large meal before sweat bathing puts a strain

on the circulatory system. It is best to wait an hour or two after a large meal before participating in a sweat lodge.

• Remove jewelry and glasses before entering the sweat lodge. Metal can get burning hot, and heat causes capillaries and skin to swell making rings and bracelets tight and constricting. Most people leave these things on the altar prior to entering the sweat lodge.

• Remove contact lenses before entering the sweat lodge since the heat can cause them to dry out and cause eye irritation.

• Move slowly as you crawl out of the sweat lodge. Fainting may occur if you stand up too abruptly. In fact, it is a good idea to simply crawl out of the lodge and lie on the ground for a moment or two, then sit up for a few moments before standing up. Blood vessels relax in the heat and when you stand up too suddenly, blood rushes down, depriving the head of blood causing faintness.

• People who not accustomed to the heat may feel nauseous. This nausea is caused by a lack of blood to the parasympathetic nervous system and is a warning sign that you are about to faint. This can also result from sweating on an empty stomach resulting in low blood sugar. Leave the sweat lodge if you feel nauseous, lie down and if possible have someone bring you fruit juice. The sugar in the fruit juice will raise your blood sugar quickly and will help relieve the nausea.

• Relaxing in the sweat lodge is very strenuous activity. The heat acts like a fever and causes every organ in your body to leap into action cleaning out toxins from your body. While outwardly relaxed, your inner organs are as active as though you were working out. This internal cleaning is a good thing, but if you are not accustomed to working out you might find that you need to leave the sweat lodge early. Remember to listen to your body. Everyone reacts differently to heat. Let your body tell you when it has had enough, don't force yourself to endure unbearable heat. Your body will gradually adapt with repeated exposure to heat in future sweat lodges. Your sweat will flow more readily and your cardiovascular system will function and cool more efficiently, but initially it is important to take it easy.

• Hot steam can scorch skin and lungs. The amount of water that is poured on the rocks controls the heat in the sweat lodge. Lots of water creates lots of steam which makes for a very hot sweat lodge, but it cools down more quickly. Less water results in a cooler sweat lodge, but it retains the heat longer. Native warriors would call out for more water as a way of showing how tough they were, but they were very experienced at sweating, for most of us it is best to go easy with the dipper.

• Be very careful when bringing the hot stones into the sweat lodge. Don't let them roll out of the pit. Also, be careful not to bring any burning coals from the fire into the lodge, the smoke from the burning coals will make it difficult to breath.

The sweat lodge and healing

All these previous warnings make participating in a sweat lodge sound like a dangerous thing, but for most people throughout history sweat bathing was considered a powerful remedy for many ailments, both physical and mental. I do not think that sweat baths would have been given such cultural importance all over the world if they had not been proven to serve humankind in practical ways.

The sweat lodge cleans your body in ways that no other bath can. You are cleansed from the inside out.

The physical benefits of sweating

Because of its ability to eliminate waste, the skin is sometimes called the third kidney. Death by toxic poisoning will occur in a matter of hours if the skin and sweat passages are smothered.

Sweating helps to rid the body of wastes. Most of us do not sweat enough. A sedentary life style combined with the use of antiperspirants results in sluggish, plugged up sweat glands that do not operate efficiently. Sweat bathing can open clogged skin pores and stimulate the healthy flow of sweat. Depending upon the individual, during a typical sweat lodge ceremony approximately one quart of sweat is excreted.

Some studies indicate that half an hour of sweating can flush more toxic metals such as copper, lead, zinc, and mercury from the body than the kidneys can handle in 24 hours. In Finland the sauna is often recommended as a supplement to kidney machines.

Sweating can facilitate the release of excess salts, a factor associated with hypertension. Doctors in Europe often prescribe sweat bathing for patients with mild hypertension, while doctors in North America continue to discourage sweat bathing for their patients.

Sweating can also draw lactic acid out of the system. Lactic acid is responsible for stiff muscles and contributes to general fatigue.

During the sweat lodge the surface temperature of the skin can rise by as much as 10 degrees C, and the inner temperature of the body increases up to 3 degrees C. This results in an artificial "fever" that is believed to cure diseases.

Aboriginal people may not have known exactly why this worked, but through observation they found it to be effective. We now know that many bacteria and viruses do not survive at temperatures higher than normal body temperature. It could also be that damaged cells repair themselves more quickly in fever conditions due to the increased metabolic rate.

Sweating regulates your body temperature

Taking part in a sweat lodge ceremony in cold weather results in a warm glowing feeling that lingers for hours afterwards, while paradoxically, in hot weather, the body seems cooler afterwards.

I am not really sure how this works. I have been told that it has something to do with the skin's ability to use sweating to regulate body temperature. But, I have also heard that it is because of the effect of the heat on the endocrine glands, the pituitary gland in particular. The pituitary is known as the master gland because it regulates both metabolism and the activity of the other glands such as the thyroid, adrenal, ovaries and testes. Stimulated by the heat, the pituitary accelerates the body's metabolism and affects the interplay of several of the body's hormones resulting in feeling warmer in cold temperatures and cooler in hotter temperatures.

Although I do not know exactly how and why this works, I know from my own experience that it does work.

Stings and bites

In the past, sweat bathing was the only effective treatment for poisonous stings or bites. I certainly don't recommend that you run for the sweat lodge rather than the doctor if you have gotten a poisonous bite, but it does seem to help relieve the swelling and itching of mosquito and black fly bites.

The healing properties of willow

In a healing sweat lodge some people choose to put willow in the water in order to benefit from its healing properties. Willow is a wonderful gift from the Creator. Willow bark contains salicin, which is a painkiller and the effective ingredient in aspirin. It is also a blood thinner and is used extensively for the prevention of heart attacks. A very versatile plant, there are many other ailments for which willow and aspirin are effective.

Arthritis/rheumatism

Warming the aching limbs with heat and steam is a traditional Native American treatment for arthritis and rheumatism. Medicinal herbs such as willow were put in the water and the water was splashed on the rocks, poured on the aching limb, and drunk by the sufferer.

Headaches

A traditional Native American treatment for headaches involves putting dry herbs and flowers on hot stones and inhaling the fumes.

Women's health

Traditionally, in most Native American tribes women were not required to take part in sweat lodge ceremonies, because it was believed that their menstrual cycle served to purify them and connect them with Mother Earth, and also because it was believed that women in their "moon time" (menstruation) were too powerful and their energy would overpower that of the men. Post-menopausal women could participate though.

However this does not mean that women could not use the sweat lodge for their own spiritual and healing purposes. It is not uncommon for groups of women living in close proximity to find that their menstrual cycles align with the others in the group. Often special "moon lodges" would be held when several women were menstruating. In addition to the spiritual and social aspects of this type of sweat lodge, it also helped to alleviate the discomfort of menstrual cramps through relaxation and the removal of excess fluid caused by sodium retention.

Participating in a sweat lodge during pregnancy and following childbirth would help to relieve aching muscles, cleanse the body, and facilitate recovery. In Finland many women believe that the heat of the sauna promotes the breast's ability to produce milk.

The sweat lodge is believed to be useful in easing menopausal symptoms by stimulating the autonomic nervous system, the pituitary gland, the adrenal glands and the ovaries. Some theories suggest that the unpleasant symptoms of menopause such as hot flashes and mood swings are an elimination issue, that menstruation does more than simply eliminate the uterine lining; that it is an elimination cycle for the entire body. When the woman's menstrual cycle stops the body must find other ways of ridding itself of toxic accumulations. While this adjustment is taking place, uncomfortable menopause symptoms are felt. Releasing this toxic buildup through sweating helps to alleviate these symptoms.

Negative ions

Science has now proven what primitive peoples knew instinctively, that water vapor has healing powers.

Some of these healing powers can be attributed to the production of negative ions. Ions play an important role in how our bodies function and in how we feel. Research has shown that an abundance of negative ions in the air is beneficial, while a higher ratio of positive ions to negative ions (positive ion poisoning) causes us to become anxious, fatigued and tense and has been linked to heart attacks, asthma, migraine headaches, insomnia, rheumatism, arthritis, hay fever, and allergies. Positive ion poisoning can be caused by weather disturbances, central air conditioning, air pollution and spending too much time confined in a closed automobile.

Negative ion therapy has been used effectively to treat burns, respiratory ailments, infections, and even to slow the spread of cancer.

An ion is a molecule with an electric charge, either positive or negative. Ionization is the process of converting a molecule into an ion by adding or removing charged particles. Ionization takes place when some force acts on a molecule and causes an electron to break away. Since electrons are negatively charged, the molecule which has lost an electron has a greater positive charge -- a positive ion. The lost electron then moves around freely until it attaches itself to another molecule causing the new molecule to become negatively charged -- a negative ion.

Most ionization takes place naturally as a result of radiation in the earth's crust and cosmic rays, but tests have shown that fire, moving water (like water falls and ocean surf), plants, and splashing water on super-heated rocks in a sweat lodge can also create an abundance of negative ions in the air.

In conclusion

Throughout history, sweat bathing has been considered a powerful remedy for many ailments, both physical and mental. I do not think that it would have had such universal acceptance if it did not have some proven beneficial effects.

The important thing is to listen to your body, and not overdo it. Remember, the sweat lodge is not intented as a form of self abuse, nor is it a substitute for medical care. If you have specific medical concerns see your doctor.

Lessons From the Sweat Lodge

8

People repeatedly ask me what is so special about the sweat lodge. What is so profound about sweating in the dark, often with a bunch of strangers? This is a question that is difficult to answer because what you experience is so personal and so profound, that when you try to explain it in the cool light of day outside of the sweat lodge it sounds so trivial.

The sweat lodge teaches different lessons to each of us, and no matter how many times you participate in one you always learn something new. The lesson it teaches us is always exactly the right one for the moment.

Fear

Anyone who has ever participated in a sweat lodge understands that the sweat lodge is a place of testing. There are moments when you think that you cannot stand it a moment longer and that you have to get out. Your fears intensify your discomfort, but if you can get past your fears you will learn some important things about yourself.

Fear serves an important purpose, it keeps us safe in

dangerous situations, but fear can also be our worst enemy, by keeping us locked away in our own little box, afraid to try new things, afraid to change.

It is human nature to fear the things we do not understand, but this fear must be overcome if we are to grow and become the person that we were meant to be. How can we overcome fear? By learning more about the thing we fear. The sweat lodge can help because it forces us to face our fears. The stifling heat and the darkness of the sweat lodge can bring to the surface fears that we didn't even realize that we had.

We all have fears, but often our fears are irrational. For example, many people are afraid of the dark. Our logical mind reminds us that there is nothing in the darkness that wasn't already there before we turned out the lights, but still we are afraid.

We are either repelled by or attracted to what we fear; the appeal that amusement park rides like roller coasters offers is the sensation of fear that riders experience. It seems that many people who are frightened of dark, enclosed spaces seem to be drawn to the sweat lodge like moths to a flame.

Fear of change

We all fear change. Sometimes we feel that things would be so much more comfortable if they would just stay they way they are, but that is not going to happen. At this point in history our entire planet is in the midst of dramatic changes, both climatic and social, and the fear of change is causing pain for many. What we have to understand is that change is inevitable, we cannot hold it off. We can try digging in our heels but that just makes it more painful when we are swept away by forces beyond our control. Everything in life is either growing or decaying, there is no standing still. You see this in the cycles of nature and you see it in the work place, either you are advancing (growing), or you are on your way out the door (decaying).

Our bodies are continually changing from the time of conception to beyond death. We like to think that if we exercise and eat right we can hold back the ravages of time, but that is just an illusion. In general, human beings fear death. Death is something that will happen to all of us at some point, we cannot expect to escape it, so why do we fear it? We fear it because we do not understand it, none of us have ever really experienced death, and we don't really know what to expect. Death is some dark void that you enter and never come back from. For some people the darkness of the sweat lodge highlights their fear of death.

Prior to my first sweat lodge I had many fears about the experience, primarily irrational physical fears. Watching all the slim, limber people milling around, people who seemed to know what they were doing, I almost backed out. Would I be able to stand the heat, would I be able to sit on the ground for so long without getting leg cramps, would I be able to crawl into the lodge, would I be able to get out of the lodge and stand up afterward, would I do something inappropriate because I wasn't familiar with sweat lodge etiquette? But my biggest fear of all, would I be embarrassed by asking to leave the lodge early?

At this point I had two choices, back away and tell myself that I didn't care about doing a sweat lodge, tell myself that there was nothing special about the sweat lodge ceremony that I couldn't achieve through meditation, and possibly miss something incredible, or face my fears, be willing to possibly be embarrassed, and go for it.

I am so glad that, in this case, I didn't let my fears hold me back. That first sweat lodge taught me three important lessons:

1) What you focus on grows
2) Live in the moment
3) You are stronger than you think

What you focus on grows

For me, the realization that "what you focus on grows" was a profound, life-altering change. Sure, I was familiar with the concept that the world is what you think it is, that all things begin with thought, and that thoughts manifest themselves into reality. I was an avid reader of Florence Scovel-Shinn's wonderful little book *The Game of Life and How to Play It*, so I thought I understood this. I understood it intellectually, but it wasn't until I experienced it so dramatically in the sweat lodge that I really knew it to be true.

I was sitting in the sweat lodge during the second endurance. My legs were numb, my butt was sore, I was drenched in sweat. It seemed unendurably hot. It was becoming more unbearable by the moment. I didn't think I would be able to last much longer.

Without my saying anything, the leader understood what I was feeling, and he told me to just focus on the drumming. Up until that moment I had been focusing on the unpleasant sensations, and as a result they were increasing by the moment. When I began to ignore them and focused my attention solely on the rhythm of the drum beat the unpleasant sensations began to lose intensity and disappear. As if by magic, the temperature in the sweat lodge got cooler, and my breathing became much easier. By focusing my attention exclusively on "living in the moment" feeling the drum beat, instead of projecting unpleasant thoughts about the future I was able to change the experience. I remember thinking, 'WOW this really works'. I realize that it sounds so trivial, but for me it was a transforming experience.

The concept of "what you focus on grows" applies to both positive and negative thoughts, and small items as well as large. With that in mind, it is important to be conscious of what you spend your time thinking about. Any time you think about something you are devoting energy to it and are creating it in your mind. Once you create it in your mind it will eventually appear in your outer world.

If you want to change something in your life simply focus on the thing that you want, not on what you don't want. Ignore what you don't want and it will disappear. If you want a happy relationship focus on what you enjoy about your partner and ignore the traits that you don't like and in time the negative traits will disappear, or at least you won't notice them, and in the meantime you will feel happier.

The time and energy you devote to worrying about the bad things that might happen in the future, only helps to bring them closer to reality. Control your thoughts and you control your world.

I now endeavor to refuse to think about or discuss anything that I do not want to experience either for myself or for someone else. This isn't always easy for me to do, I'm no different than anyone else, but after seeing how dramatically our thoughts can change our circumstances I try to catch myself if I find myself worrying about future events or speculating (gossiping) about someone else's situation.

The world is what you think it is

So, was that particular sweat lodge an unbearably hot endurance test, or was it an exhilarating opportunity to participate in group chanting, drumming, and meditation? I have come to really understand that everything in the world is exactly what we think it is at that moment. Everything begins with our thoughts and our interpretation of the events around us. Our thoughts and our self-talk determine whether we experience happiness or sorrow, pleasure or pain.

All the events in our lives are interpreted through the filter of our experiences and beliefs. Have you ever noticed how when you buy a new car of a particular make and color suddenly you start seeing that same make and color of car wherever you go? It is not that suddenly the car dealerships had a run on blue Toyota Corolla's, it is just that now you have started to notice what was already there in front of you that you just didn't see before.

If we choose to believe that the world is a kind, loving place we will notice those things that support this belief and tend to fail to notice anything that contradicts it. On the other hand if you choose to believe that the world and everyone in it are evil and dangerous you will soon find plenty of evidence to support that belief. Since we can find plenty of evidence to support either of these beliefs it is up to us to decide which belief will create the kind of experience that we want to have. Which belief serves us better? Which belief makes us happier?

There are no limits, everything is possible

If my mind can effectively change my experience of the temperature of the sweat lodge what else can it affect? Our minds are far more powerful than we realize, and we have not even begun to tap into its power.

Is it possible to use the power of your mind to affect others? Yes definitely. When the sweat lodge leader reminded me to focus on the drumming he helped to positively transform my experience.

We have all experienced how infectious emotions can be. One person with a negative attitude can drag everyone around them down into their despair, and yet we have also experienced how another person's optimistic outlook can elevate the mood of everyone around them. Do you want to be remembered as someone who made everyone around them miserable, or would you prefer to help people around you feel good?

I think it is possible for a critical mass of people to influence events for either good or bad through the power of their minds. When enough people begin to think the same way things change. Look at the changes in North American society in the last 50 years. The civil rights movement which began back in the 1950's, the Gay Pride movement which began in the late 1960's are two examples of how a critical mass of people were able to radically transform society's notions of what is acceptable and appropriate within a relatively short period of time.

Living in the moment

Living in the moment is a concept that is difficult for many of us. We spend most of our time dreaming about and planning for events in the future, or regretting events in the past, when really the only time that we have control of is the present. We need to remember that our life is a series of present moments, the past is gone and the future may never come. Our thoughts and actions in the present are what determine our future.

You are stronger than you think

Conquering your fears and completing a sweat lodge ceremony is an exhilarating experience, by facing your greatest enemy - yourself, you see that you really are stronger than you think.

Before I went into my first sweat lodge I was afraid that I would end up disrupting the ceremony by needing to leave. I had been comparing myself to all the other people about to enter the lodge and thinking that they all looked much more physically fit than me, and with their feathers, and other spiritual accoutrements they appeared so much more "spiritual" than me. Like anyone else, I hate to be embarrassed, and I was afraid that I was about to make a fool of myself, but something inside me nudged me on.

The first endurance had barely begun when a man began panicking and asked to be let out, followed shortly by two women. I remember feeling relieved (and a little bit smug) that others had given up while I was still toughing it out, but then I realized that I was judging them unfairly since I do not understand their journey, I do not understand what demons they were struggling with, and perhaps if I had been in their situations I would have needed to leave the sweat lodge early too.

The sweat lodge is not a competition. Yes, it is a time of discomfort and testing, but you do not need to prove anything to anyone but yourself. What you experience is between you and the Creator.

When the ceremony was completed and we all crawled out of the sweat lodge I felt so proud of myself, I had made it. It really did demonstrate to me that I was stronger than I thought I was. How many other things in my life had I been reluctant to try due to irrational fears?

Subsequent sweat lodges have taught me many other lessons.

The sweat lodge as a spiritual journey

The sweat lodge represents our spiritual journey. Different parts of the ceremony teach us different things. Gathering the willow for the frame, the wood for the fire, the rocks to be heated and the water to create the steam reminds us that we are all interconnected and that we depend on others as we struggle through life. The hard work of gathering the materials reminds us that to be successful requires effort on our part. Crawling into the sweat lodge teaches us humility, the interior of the sweat lodge represents the womb of Mother Earth, its darkness represents human ignorance.

We are stronger together

Sitting on the ground looking up at the sweat lodge frame we see thin flexible saplings which, when tied together in a grid, create a strong frame. We are reminded that when we join together with others we are stronger together than we are separately. The cross pieces of the sweat lodge frame remind us that when we join together with others who are different from us (have different perspectives) if we are flexible and work together we become stronger.

This is the idea behind marriage or business partnerships. When two people who have different strengths and perspectives come together and work as a team they can accomplish far more than one person alone can possibly accomplish.

The unseen world around us

I have been in sweat lodges where startling images appeared in the heated rocks, where tiny spirit lights began sparkling inside the total darkness of the lodge, where wild animals circled around outside the lodge, all things that are outside of our usual experience.

These odd events take place to show us that there is far more going on around us than we can see or understand with our human senses. The Elders taught that this physical world that we live in is just a shadow of the "real" world to come, and these unexplained phenomena that sometimes take place in the sweat lodge remind us of this.

Effectiveness is the measure of truth

Every religion claims to have the "truth", but what is "true"? The real measure of "truth" is whether it "works" for you. Does what you believe help you, does it give you comfort, make you a better, kinder individual? In the sweat lodge so much of what we learn is personal and private, and since our spiritual or religious beliefs can never be completely "proven", if a ritual or a belief is effective for you, then it is true for you.

All power comes from within

The Elders taught that the Great Spirit is not some external force. It is inside all of us, surrounding all of us, and connecting all of us. We already have all the power that we need to change ourselves and anything about our surroundings. The sweat lodge can give us a glimpse of our personal power.

Intention is everything

It is not enough to simply participate in some ritual, the magic is not in the ritual itself, rather the magic is in our intention. In all spiritual activities our intention is the crucial ingredient. If we are sincere in our desire to grow spiritually, the sweat lodge ritual can help.

In Conclusion -- We are all related

The sweat lodge reminds us that we are dependent upon each other and on Mother Earth for our survival. As Chief Seattle said, "All things share the same breath - the beast, the tree, the man... the air shares its spirit with all the life it supports... All things are bound together, all things connect".

We are all related, and can all benefit from what the sweat lodge offers us.

Index

To discover more books about
personal development, spirituality
and divination visit:

www.learnancientwisdom.com

To learn more about the author visit:
www.irenemcgarvie.com